Effective
Internal
Communication

To the late Ian Connell,
without whom this book would never have been possible

PR IN PRACTICE SERIES

Effective Internal Communication

Lyn Smith
with Pamela Mounter

CHARTERED INSTITUTE OF PUBLIC RELATIONS

KOGAN
PAGE

London and Sterling, VA

First published in Great Britain and the United States in 2005 by Kogan Page Limited

120 Pentonville Road
London N1 9JN
United Kingdom
www.kogan-page.co.uk

22883 Quicksilver Drive
Sterling VA 20166-2012
USA

© Lyn Smith, 2005

ISBN 0 7494 3948 3

British Library Cataloguing-in-Publication Data

A CIP record for this book is available from the British Library.

Library of Congress Cataloging-in-Publication Data

Smith, Lyn.
   Effective internal communication / Lyn Smith.
       p. cm. — (PR in practice series)
   Includes bibliographical references and index.
   ISBN 0-7494-3948-3
   1. Communication in management. 2. Public relations. I. Title. II.
Series.
HD30.3.S577 2005
658.4′5—dc22

                                                            2005012626

Typeset by JS Typesetting Ltd, Porthcawl, Mid Glamorgan
Printed and bound in Great Britain by Creative Print and Design (Wales), Ebbw Vale

Contents

PR in Practice Series

**Published in association with the Chartered Institute of Public Relations
Series Editors: Anne Gregory and Gro Elin Hansen**

Kogan Page has joined forces with the Chartered Institute of Public Relations to publish
this unique series which is designed specifically to meet the needs of the increasing
numbers of people seeking to enter the public relations profession and the large band
of existing PR professionals. Taking a practical, action-oriented approach, the books in
the series concentrate on the day-to-day issues of public relations practice and
management rather than academic history. They provide ideal primers for all those on
CIPR, CAM and CIM courses or those taking NVQs in PR. For PR practitioners, they
provide useful refreshers and ensure that their knowledge and skills are kept up to
date.

Anne Gregory is one of the UK's leading public relations academics. She is Director of
the Centre for Public Relations Studies at Leeds Metropolitan University. Before
becoming an academic, Anne spent 12 years in public relations practice and has
experience at a senior level both in-house and in consultancy. She remains involved in
consultancy work and is a non-executive director of South West Yorkshire Mental health
NHS Trust with special responsibility for communication issues. Anne is Consultant
Editor of the PR in Practice series and edited the book of the same name and wrote and
Planning and Managing a Public Relations Campaign, also in this series. She was President
of the CIPR in 2004.

Gro Elin Hansen is the in-house Editor of the PR in Practice series, as well as being
Editor of *Profile*, the Chartered Institute of Public Relations' member magazine.

Other titles in the series:

Creativity in Public Relations by Andy Green
Effective Media Relations by Michael Bland, Alison Theaker and David Wragg
Effective Writing Skills for Public Relations by John Foster
Managing Activism by Denise Deegan
Online Public Relations by David Phillips
Planning and Managing Public Relations Campaigns by Anne Gregory
Public Relations in Practice edited by Anne Gregory
Public Relations Strategy by Sandra Oliver
Public Relations: A practical guide to the basics by Philip Henslowe
Risk Issues and Crisis Management in Public Relations by Michael Regester and Judy Larkin
Running a Public Relations Department by Mike Beard

Forthcoming titles:

Introduction to Public Affairs by Stuart Thompson and Dr Steve John

The above titles are available from all good bookshops and from the CIPR website
www.cipr.co.uk/books   To obtain further information, please contact the publishers at
the address below:

Kogan Page Ltd
120 Pentonville Road
London N1 9JN
Tel: 020 7278 0433 Fax: 020 7837 6348
www.kogan-page.co.uk

About the author

Lyn Smith has worked as a professional communicator for the bulk of her 30-year career starting out in film publicity, moving to internal communication in a commercial organization, copywriting and media relations for a direct marketing agency, and later professional institute public relations.

She then changed direction and moved into newspaper journalism, becoming responsible for a news team of 15 before returning to public relations, this time in the National Health Service. From there she set up her own public relations consultancy and has worked in all sectors, most recently working with a wide range of not-for-profit organizations.

She has also worked as chief executive of a charity for health and social care professionals and has lectured on public relations.

A Fellow of the Chartered Institute of Public Relations, from 1999 until 2005 she chaired the sectoral group for the not-for-profit sector, Fifth Estate, quadrupling its membership. She was previously secretary of the institute's Internal Communication Group. She is a member of a number of other institutes and organizations including the RSA.

Lyn has edited a number of professional journals including the *British Journal of Healthcare Computing and Information Management* and the UK Centre for the Advancement of Interprofessional Education's *Bulletin*.

Educational qualifications include the CAM certificate and diploma and an MA in Communications Planning.

About the editor

Pamela Mounter is a senior corporate communication consultant. A childhood in Africa and postings to Europe and the Caucasus developed her interest in the influence of culture on the way people relate to each other. She has written about internal communication for both academic and general publications and won a top paper award from the International Association of Business Communicators for her work with BP in this area. She is a member of the Thames Valley University advisory committee for its MSc in Corporate Communication and a committee member of the Chartered Institute of Public Relations' International Group.

Acknowledgements

This book was only made possible by the vast number of contributions which largely came in the form of interviews and in some cases submitted materials.

I would particularly like to thank the following, who are not listed according to merit: Gerald Chan, Gro Elin Hansen, the late Alan Rawel and Susan Shayshutt of the Chartered Institute of Public Relations; Amanda Foister, Internal Communication Alliance; Professor Anne Gregory; Pamela Mounter; Dr Richard Varey.

For their contributions: Lesley Allman, Coors Brewers; David Ashford, Lloyds TSB; Michelle Atkinson, North Tees and Hartlepool NHS Trust; Sophie Austin, IBM; David Barker, British Heart Foundation; Caroline Bramley, Flag; Caroline Broadhurst, TDM; Paul Brown, The Princes Trust; David Bryant, BUPA; Liz Cochrane, Work Foundation; David Coe, Media Maker; Jonathan Coe, LE Group; Denice Currie, Norwich Union; Aniko Czinege, Amersham Biosciences; Siubhan Daly, VisitScotland; Vicki Davies, National Blood Service; Sue Dewhurst, NTL; Elizabeth Dickie, Cable & Wireless; Arfon Edward, Quadrant PR; Lindsay Eynon, Hill & Knowlton; Colin Farrington, Chartered Institute of Public Relations; Simon Finn, Safeway; Liam Fitzpatrick, ICA; James Flynn, Marina Pirotta Communication; Richard Gaunt; Helen Goodier, Chandler Gooding; Russell Grossman, BBC; Justine Guest, Trinity Management Consultancy; Katie Hadgraft, Cable & Wireless; Johnny Harben; Tom Harvey, Nationwide; Shiona Hastie, Customs & Excise; Nick Helsby, Watson Helsby; Sarah

Hoskins, DaimlerChrysler; Paul Inglefield, Adur District Council; Rachel Jefferies, Questions of Difference; Norma Johnston, Plan; Stephen Jolly; Jill Kirby, Lloyds TSB; Howard Krais, Eversheds; Briony Lalor, AA; Peter Lawlor, Hill & Knowlton; Carol Lindsell; Simon Loe, Lucent Technologies; Richard Lomax, Redhouse Lane; Judith Manson, VisitScotland; Paul Massie; Mike McCabe, Buckinghamshire County Council; Karen McElroy, Coors Brewers; Lisa Moore, The Children's Society; Mike Moser, Rio Tinto; Sarah Murphy, Capital One Bank; Sidonie Myers, Smith and Nephew; Alexander Nicoll, Church of England Archbishops' Council; Grace Perrott, Allied Irish Banks; David Phillips; Ellie Phillips, West Wiltshire Housing Society; Robert Pike; Jacqui Price, Jeremy Redhouse, Redhouse Lane; Jane Relf, Vertex; James Rye, The Disabilities Trust; Jo Sanders, Olswang; Emma Savage, Barclays; Bob Schukai, Motorola; Colin Sneath, Credo; Leslie Sophocleous; Phil Talbot, NSPCC; Steve Taylor, Sue Ryder Care; Mandy Thatcher, Melcrum Publishing; Susan Walker, MORI; Jenny Waller; Sandra Ward, BMW Hams Hall; Sarah Watson, Dogs for the Disabled; Clare Winterton, The Princes Trust; Nick Wright, Fishburn Hedges; Oliver Wright, Shelter; Stephen Windsor-Lewis, BAE Systems; Fiona Young, Hill & Knowlton.

Introduction

Sharpening my pencil (pens had a habit of running ink in the rain, and juggling an umbrella, pen and notebook was just not one of my special competencies), I prepared to conduct yet another interview in my busy working day as a local newspaper reporter. Being no more callous than any other hack (this was the early 1980s) I conducted the interview with the boss of one of the largest factories in the area and then processed back to the office to provide the front page lead for the main newspaper of the week.

My sense of revelation came when I did my weekly session with scissors and glue pot to keep my cuttings book up to date and reread those words: 'Four hundred jobs to go'. There had been no trade union representative to speak to, to get the other side of the story. We had taken the word of the managers and committed the information to black and white type set in the old-fashioned way in hot metal.

Within a few months that technology would be swept away but what did not vanish, as I was to note down the years, was a tendency to use the nearest journalist to inform staff that the P45 was in the post and that despite 30 years service they were no longer required.

My first role after newspapers was in heading up the communications function for an inner London health district. By then I had realized that I had grown tired of having little impact; a newspaper journalist is essentially an outsider looking in, and I wanted to make an impact by being on the inside looking and communicating out.

A review of my cuttings had revealed that apart from the bad news stories, very few of the 72-point headlines had been much more than 'flying kites' for various proposals that had never come to anything. Working from the inside of an organization I had hoped to make a real difference to the way its employees were treated, and the way they in turn would treat the 'customers', as patients had by then been rechristened.

I was operating against a backdrop of major and continuing change. In the Mental Health Unit in particular, employees had undergone a number of changes in top management. They also had to face the effects of the then Tory government reforms which effectively divorced them from the other health provider units. However, by ensuring their voices were heard through the communications vehicles and so responded to by senior management, the transfer of services from institution to community went gratifyingly well.

In the 15 years or so since I moved back into the corporate sector and then on into consultancy, things appear to have changed pretty dramatically in the world of internal communication. Few organizations of any size will not now be devoting time, money and resources to internal audiences as well as what have been viewed as the rather more supposedly glamorous external ones.

But why do internal communications at all? The reason they do so is because an informed and engaged workforce produces better results. Unless your people understand what your organization is seeking to achieve and the part they have to play, arriving at your hoped-for corporate destination will not be a foregone conclusion.

Few communicators and their counterparts in human resources feel comfortable putting figures on the impact that their efforts may have on the corporate profit and loss account. However, communication is not just about bolstering the bottom line: it can assist in other areas that impact upon the health of the organization.

Your workforce can serve as ambassadors in both positive and negative respects. Poor handling of complaints regarding racial harassment and discrimination have often found their way to an employment tribunal. An internal communicator with the ear of senior management can sound the alarm or at least advise on how to communicate an effective solution.

Damning headlines can in themselves be very damaging for employee morale. It is vital for both internal and external communications functions to be aligned or at least working closely together. It is only too easy for internally generated media to find its way to the outside world and so influence external perceptions, and external media can often be the first port of call for staff looking for company news.

It has always seemed common sense and good etiquette to talk to your internal publics first before going to the wider world, although it is vital to remember that the Stock Exchange requires to be informed of price-sensitive information in advance.

Professional communicators are also in the ideal position to translate 'management speak' into language that can be understood by those who will have to act upon it.

All organizations have their own cultures, and when two organizations try to merge, the importance of those cultures comes to the fore. By culture I mean the patterns of behaviour and attitudes exhibited by employees and management. Again professional communicators attuned to the sensitivities that abound can help overcome the barriers to happy corporate marriage.

All the above perhaps suggests that the only time to keep in touch with staff is in periods of stress or trouble. In fact, if you maintain contact in a regular pattern at regular times it is more likely that the workforce will want to pull together when the going does get rough.

Communicating clear goals and then reporting on progress at regular intervals is motivating for teams. Activity for publics both internal and external should be closely matched to organizational targets. There is a hierarchy of communication needs, from 'How do I fit into my team?' to 'Where does the team fit into this part of the organization?' to 'And how does that fit into the big picture?' Internal communications should meet all those needs. Being able to see exactly how an individual contributes to the bigger picture is the key not just for management but also for motivating the individual concerned.

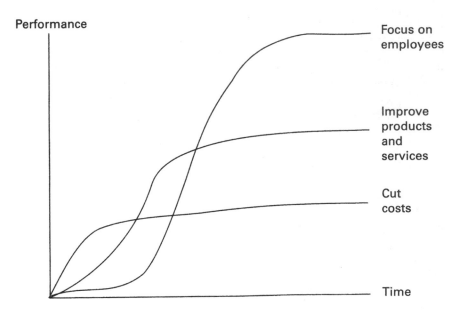

Figure 0.1 *Sources of performance improvement – the business case for internal communication*

Sources of performance improvement

So, any conclusions? Internal communications is still relatively new as a function but is by and large better developed in the commercial sector. However, the public sector is catching up fast and, like the not-for-profit sector, may be pulling ahead in terms of employee engagement. It is much easier to embrace the vision of helping a community than selling a biscuit, no matter how healthy.

The not-for-profit sector may be seen to be lagging behind, but this may be more to do with the size and age of the organization in question as few in the sector employ large numbers of staff. Available budgets are also obviously a contributory factor. It can still be hard to justify investment on staff when donors want to see money spent on the worthy cause itself. But more and more communications posts are being advertised, so this will change.

Looking across all sectors it would seem that size of organization rather than sector is the determining factor. Large organizations, certainly in the public and commercial sectors, will quite naturally be better resourced and better able to take advantage of new technological advances and societal developments as they come on stream. However, all organizations with just 50 or more employees will be obliged to take account of the strictures of the European Commission's Information and Consultation Directive (see Chapter 7).

This book is intended to help those out in the field to learn from the real experiences of the very many people I have spoken to, working across all sectors and sizes of organizations. Although theory will be touched on in the first half, this book is as much about the reality and practice of internal communication. The practicalities of internal communication are covered from Chapter 13. A skills matrix is provided in Appendix 1, and full references plus further reading are supplied.

Part 1

Setting the Scene

1

What is internal communication?

Or should that be 'internal communications', or for that matter 'staff communications' or 'employee relations', or if you are a real dinosaur 'industrial relations'? Perhaps if you are somewhat more up to date you might prefer 'change management'. The list is pretty extensive or would be if you trawled back through the recruitment section of the *Guardian*. This chapter will first look at what internal communication is and then move on to look at the make-up of the internal communicator.

What's in a name? The same arguments have presumably been played out over that equally aged moniker for our external-facing colleagues – very few seem to be called press officers these days. In fact that is a bit of a misnomer as they often have to conduct government affairs, community relations and marketing communications, along with media relations too; internal communication is a small but significant part of their work.

Speaking in October 2002 at the launch of the Internal Communication Alliance, Chair Stephen Windsor-Lewis said the discipline had 'come a long way'. He described it as 'an essential element in the business mix'.

Stephen Windsor-Lewis added the term 'leadership communications' to the list of alternative terms for internal communication. It is likely this phrase has come into play due to the focus on Britain's perceived lack of leadership skills, as commented on in reports from the Council for Excellence in Management and Leadership (Fox *et al*, 2001; Perren and

Grant, 2001). It might therefore be seen as focusing on the needs of the boardroom or perhaps providing the workforce with something more than the usual top-down exhortations.

What exactly is meant by each of these phrases could fill a volume on its own. At the BBC they see 'internal communication' as the act of communicating internally, while 'internal communications' is the function which helps deliver it. There are of course other interpretations, but this book does not intend to enter into a debate on the subject although it recognizes that there are differing points of view.

If nothing else, that trawl through the Appointments section does provide a barometer for how far the discipline has grown. Internal communication is now a long way from the days when it was something to be fitted in around external affairs duties. Nowadays even charities, not known for their vast budgets, can consider establishing stand-alone functions, whereas teams in supposedly rather better resourced sectors have usually gone from one to many members of staff; but in some instances the reverse appears to be the case. This perhaps serves to highlight yet another phase of the discipline's development from producer to adviser.

In some ways, looking at the manner in which different sectors and/or different sizes of organizations are currently managing or carrying out the function of internal communication provides a series of snapshots of the way the discipline has been maturing. There would seem no better way of finding the future path than learning from those who have gone before.

THE HISTORY

Smaller organizational decisions should be taken by senior individuals, but large ones should be decided as a group. Everyone's voice must be heard to avoid murmurs and back-biting.

Those words were not written some time in that great age of internal communication, the 20th century, but in the 6th century by a monk. In an article entitled 'The spirit of enterprise' published in the *Daily Telegraph*, 16 November 2000, Widget Finn could see the relevance of St Benedict's Rule at the dawning of the new millennium.

St Benedict's successors now use his words as the basis for weekend retreats for business people in search of spirituality at work. Perhaps a little flippantly, it could be argued that internal communication far predates St Benedict and was probably being disseminated in pictorial form for Stone Age hunters. Who is to say those paintings of animals were not intended as an exhortation to try harder next time?

Writing in *Communication World*, Michael C Brandon (1997) cites three major phases of development but does not specifically label them; for the ease of the reader they have been roughly dated (see boxed panel). However, they could be described as: 1) industrial relations; 2) realistic journalism; and 3) marketing.

The first phase Brandon describes as the 'three Bs' or 'birthdays, babies and ballscores'; more recent efforts would perhaps slot into the 'high Cs', or 'challenge, change and commitment'. But Brandon argues that many organizations even in the dying days of the old millennium were still stuck in phases one and two.

THE EVOLUTION OF EMPLOYEE COMMUNICATIONS

Stage One (pre-1960s)

- Predecessor – industrial relations.
- Goal – improve morale.
- Emphasis – individuals.
- Orientation – camaraderie.
- Attitude – warm, personal.
- Focus – people.

Stage Two (mid-1960s–1980s)

- Predecessor – journalism.
- Goal – deliver news.
- Emphasis – facts.
- Orientation – reporting.
- Attitude – cool, sceptical.
- Focus – events.

Stage Three (late 1980s–now)

- Predecessor – marketing.
- Goal – implement strategy.
- Emphasis – organization.
- Orientation – aid to management.
- Attitude – business orientated.
- Focus – strategic objectives.

Adapted from 'From the three Bs to the high Cs', *Communication World*, April/May 1997.

While phase one was seen to be the territory of the industrial relations expert and intended to improve employees' morale by providing a source of recognition for them, phase two coincided with the influx of journalists into that part of the workforce. They brought with them the values of the newsroom and so a sharper news focus because they saw their goal as providing employees with information about their organizations. Their aspiration was to 'tell it like it is'.

Working at Albright & Wilson and Sainsbury's in the late 1960s and 1970s Richard Gaunt, under the guidance of Peter Ireson (former chairman of the old British Association of Industrial Editors), fought for and won a high degree of editorial freedom to cover often challenging subjects (from a management perspective) in equally challenging ways.

He argues this perceived freedom helped the in-house journalism team gain credibility with employees and enabled them to communicate the company's agenda very quickly and successfully. The team produced several award-winning publications. They may seem antique now, but illustrate fundamentals which have not changed. So it is likely Brandon would slot these into his second stage of development.

In producing Albright & Wilson's (then the UK's number two chemical producer) glossy magazine, the pair had the freedom to write whatever they liked as long as it was relevant to the company. Seeking to reflect the lives of employees, the publication tackled redundancy and environmental issues long before it was the fashion to do so. There was a climate of reality, openness and frankness.

They conducted interviews with trade union officials and shop stewards. This and other topics brought them into constant conflict with management but they had some strong supporters and the publication was read. At the time it was recognized as being one of the leading vehicles in employee communication.

The pair arrived at Sainsbury's when it was making the transition from a private family-owned business to a public company. They carried on their pioneering efforts by launching a four-weekly newspaper. This apparently completely changed communication in a company which had been rather hierarchical in approach and structure. There was an editorial charter along the lines of a national newspaper. According to Richard Gaunt they 'would publish and be damned and apologise afterwards but we always checked our facts'. A letters page also provided a vehicle for tackling tricky subjects. He believes the climate has changed in many companies, not necessarily for the better in terms of openness to employees.

Air Products plc launched its staff magazine in the winter of 1969 for a UK-based workforce. The 100th issue of *Cryo Gen* magazine produced early in 2003 replaced a disparate global collection of publications. Each regional edition carries a core set of pages with company information, whilst the outer pages carry locally relevant news. The first issue of the magazine was launched in the UK, Germany and Belgium with the new look being rolled out further across Europe at a later stage. Whether Redhouse Lane, the consultancy that works on it, would recognize its roots in Brandon's second phase or journalistic school of internal communication is another matter.

Working at BP in the 1970s, Pamela Mounter used a concept from more mainstream media to get the company's predominantly male audiences reading the employee newspaper. Getting a well-known face as a judge, she ran a competition to find women who were making a real contribution to BP. There were literally thousands of responses, complete with the required photographs, from the audience who then voted for the top 12 women. The winner – who just happened of course to be a pretty girl – won her own portrait to be painted by a famous artist.

Obviously rather more innocent times; and it is not easy to see such a competition winning favour today with the organization's equality or diversity officer. But at the time the device was helpful in ensuring the serious information on such issues as downsizing was read. Before the 1970s there would have been no coverage of closures.

TECHNOLOGY ADDED

Jeremy Redhouse, who set up communications consultancy Redhouse Lane in 1988, was among the pioneers of the next stage. This saw the surprisingly early adoption of video and attitude surveys which were not to be widespread for the best part of another decade. The introduction of surveys reflected a growing understanding of communications as being not just a one-way top-down process, but a two-way process at the least.

What has been interesting during conversations across the sectors is how many very large household names have only recently got around to establishing intranets. But then it is hard to grasp that they only started to become a feature of organizational life in the mid-1990s.

A survey of the sector by *PR Week* on 12 November 1992, 'Communication empowering employees', made no mention of computer-mediated communication. It divided up the internal communicator's working time into that devoted to 'mission and value statements, cascade briefs and house magazine/newspaper'.

When Corporate Communications Director Stephen Jolly first arrived at the Japanese investment bank Nomura International in 1996, the London team seemed content with a sheet of A4 detailing staff exploits. Yet the company's desire to close the perception gap between where it believed it was and where staff seemed to think it was required something far more sophisticated.

To bring together a company that had been operating as a collection of disparate businesses, all internal communication was concentrated onto a newly created intranet. For Nomura's people, their workplace was in fact the desktop computer screen through which they did their day-to-day work. The aim was to turn them into ambassadors for Nomura rather than just for the business area in which they had been operating. Without that change, the future of the organization might eventually have been put at risk.

A branding structure was needed as a framework. The individual business areas were given responsibility for intranet content. This encompassed business data as well as hard news and more light-hearted material in the form of a corporate 'webzine'. For resourcing reasons, the webzine was updated on a monthly basis in the early days, but then continuously to reflect the fast-moving nature of the financial markets. There might also have been a growing familiarity with the technology and its capabilities.

The constant reinforcement of the Nomura brand was intended to confirm for employees that they were a part of a larger corporate whole. This example ties neatly into Brandon's third or marketing stage of internal communication in his model of the evolution of employee communication. This stage has its focus on strategic objectives rather than the people and events of the first two phases.

Brandon argues that what he terms employee communications should 'evolve into an extension of the management process'. If he had updated his article for the new millennium he might have added a fourth stage. This would have built on his third stage to combine the best of all three models, with greater emphasis on listening and taking on board the contributions of the workforce.

This brings us neatly on to a brisk look at where internal communications sits within an organization.

WHERE IT SITS IN THE ORGANIZATION

Internal communications is one of those functions that everyone thinks they can do well – because they talk to their people, don't they. This can make life particularly challenging for those tasked with actually delivering on the job title they have when everyone regards the skills as commonplace.

Many interviewed for this book felt that strategy should be firmly within the remit of the in-house team or individual, otherwise a series of unlinked programmes would be the likely result.

In talking to many individuals at very different levels in very disparate sectors, what has come across as crucial is the need for internal communication to be championed at the very top of the organization. Also for senior management and the boardroom to respect the expertise of the specialist tasked to deliver, be they internally or externally placed.

Without that respect it is unlikely any communication strategy will be delivered according to plan or be effectively tied to the bottom line. Without a clear focus and understanding of expected results, the organization may well fail and certainly will not go to the top of any league tables of performance.

Since the Labour government came to power in 1997 there has been a flexing of muscle by a previously seemingly weakened trade union movement. For some this may seem to herald a return to the bad old days of the 1970s when tools were downed with alacrity. A more positive view may be that that it can emphasize the need for management to treat staff with greater respect than might have been apparent since the decline of the 'job for life' regime. The trade union representative could also be seen to provide another channel of communication to the workforce, and the European Commission's Information and Consultation Directive adds further weight to this (see Chapter 7 for more on this important issue).

As already hinted at, internal communication, although it has an arguably long and perhaps venerable history, is regarded as a relatively new discipline. There are few if any directors of internal communication sitting alongside the other directors in the boardroom, a fact borne out by the recent research by Nick Helsby in *The Rise of the Internal Communicator* (2002).

In fact, many practitioners are not accorded senior management status. This could reflect the development stage of the discipline as a whole; as the function matures its positioning within the organization should also improve.

It would appear that the majority of internal communicators report into corporate communications, which brings them alongside external communications. This gives some hope that messages are being aligned across both disciplines. Others find themselves reporting to human resources and there is another argument that this brings the individual closer to the functioning of the business itself.

Chapter 5 looks in more detail at the siting of the internal communications function. But during research for this book internal communications was found positioned in such unexpected places as administration. A positive view on this is that perhaps it does not matter where the function sits, provided it derives adequate recognition and respect and power to deliver, and that the internal communicator develops the essential links to all parts of the organization.

As the Council for Excellence in Management and Leadership has stressed in its numerous reports (Fox *et al*, 2001; Perren and Grant, 2001) leadership is needed at all levels of an organization. Line managers and supervisors, if they are to be seen to be leaders in their own right, need to know how to tell the corporate story to their teams. Internal communication can be clearly seen as part of that role. They also need to be equipped to communicate not just to but from their staff. Two-way communication is more likely to ensure the day-to-day smooth running of the organization. The ingredients required to make a good internal communicator are explored in the next chapter.

KEY POINTS TO REMEMBER

- Internal communication has moved on from events and people to sharing corporate goals.
- Internal communication needs to be championed at the very top.
- Organizations need the workforce to understand what is expected of them – internal communication will help them deliver this.
- Internal communication is still a new discipline.
- Internal communication is the responsibility of everyone from CEO to line manager and supervisor.

2

What does it take to be an internal communicator?

Structural engineering, civil engineering, comparative religion, advertising, journalism, the police, occasionally even English – just a few of the study areas, former careers and backgrounds from which internal communicators appear to come. These were just the suggestions of those talked to in the course of compiling of this book.

So what does it take to work in the internal communications function of today, and hopefully that to come? Does it require a very special kind of person or can anyone do it?

One of the most in-depth surveys of the internal communications function to date is provided by Nick Helsby (2002). Following is a concentrated look at his findings and the further comments of practitioners. A comprehensive skills matrix supplied by the Internal Communication Alliance is included in Appendix 1. The matrix establishes the skills and knowledge needed at each stage of the practitioner's career.

WHERE TO NOW FOR THE INTERNAL COMMUNICATOR?

The Watson Helsby report sought to explore the role of senior practitioners in 37 large UK and US businesses. Although this clearly focuses on the corporate sector it acts as an indicator of future trends for other sectors too.

The report takes as a given that the employer and employee relationship has changed. It asserts that the need to get employee 'buy-in' is a matter of importance to the board, and so professional internal communication is now critical for business health.

An executive search firm, Watson Helsby, conducted the research to see whether the role was gaining in complexity and influence. It also looked to see whether the skills required had changed, where practitioners could add value and whether the individuals themselves were able to take advantage of the new opportunities.

The role is described as still an immature one, and the report was intended to provide a 'route map' to show how the function could grow. Top managers have differing views on the role of internal communication, some seeing it as little more than a 'messaging service' with no particular place in the wider scheme of things, while others see it as an essential change agent.

Internal communicators can be found in human resources, corporate communication or marketing, although the research shows most sit within communications (67 per cent of those surveyed). Many feel they would be at a disadvantage and not well used if positioned in human resources or marketing. This argument is seen as rather irrelevant by the report's author, who debates that it could in fact be a 'cross-functional discipline'.

Most of those surveyed regard internal communication as having a place on the top people's agenda but often not made a priority, with most attention being paid to the external world. Holding the function back is the difficulty in putting a fiscal figure on the value of internal communication, and the lack of wider business knowledge of most practitioners.

Talent is an issue, as apparently many practitioners are at best of middling quality. But those who are good can claim salaries hitting six figures.

In the past most internal communicators have come across from broader communications but now people are coming in from brand consultancy and general management. The career path is not well designed, with many practitioners rising only to a certain level and not achieving senior management heights.

Some internal communicators do have the ear of those at the top on a regular basis, and several are involved in organizational strategy activities including culture, values and changing behaviour. Demands on the role have grown substantially.

Ways forward include the emergence of an advisory and coaching role with the emphasis on behavioural aspects and new structures that bring communication, human resources and marketing into combination.

If the holistic approach seems too radical, perhaps a pairing of human resources and marketing would create a true customer focus, whereas joining human resources and corporate communication would place the emphasis on the stakeholder.

The Watson Helsby report's author sees internal communication as having an effect on all areas of the organization. Practitioners should aim to equip themselves with the skills to get to the top and to be taken seriously by the board, and beyond their particular specialism.

The report gives a breakdown of where practitioners can currently be found in organizations, with some 67 per cent finding a niche in corporate communication, 22 per cent in human resources and 10 per cent in marketing. This does not necessarily reflect the sector as a whole as the sample was skewed towards very senior practitioners.

Corporate communication is seen as appropriate as it makes possible the alignment of internal and external communications. The human resources connection is seen as valuable in times of organizational change but otherwise not an option likely to be regarded too highly.

Marketing as a home for internal communicators made some sense in terms of the customer focus. However, this could also be seen to be to the detriment of the internally focused function, with marketing's tendency to focus on the external customer often perceived to be getting the upper hand.

Internal communication is not top of the graduates' favoured jobs list, although two-thirds of the respondents said they had made a deliberate decision to move into the role.

Again not necessarily reflective of the sector as a whole, it was found that 70 per cent of the sample believed the discipline has a strong enough voice at board or equivalent level, but it is clear from the sample that board commitment is a different issue.

The biggest obstacle to progress is the current lack of business focus, but limited resources in terms of budget and support staff ensures many practitioners are stuck in delivery rather than planning and thinking mode.

Another difficulty is that many individuals in organizations think they themselves conduct internal communication and so will not regard the internal communicator as a specialist with professional knowledge. Many respondents would like a quite different moniker as they regard 'internal communication' as obsolete and carrying negative overtones.

The roles that respondents saw for themselves included a range of both strategic and more tactical activities:

- communicating strategy;
- driving employee engagement;

- changing communications;
- design and process of communication structures including feedback;
- internalizing the brand;
- knowledge sharing;
- developing the intranet;
- leadership communication and behaviours;
- communication coaching for line managers.

The current skills set of communicators includes the following soft skills:

- influencing;
- diplomacy;
- relationship building/networking;
- listening skills;
- resilience and tenacity;
- passion and drive.

Their hard skills include:

- writing;
- media management;
- business/financial literacy;
- understanding customer focus;
- business knowledge;
- strategic insight;
- change management;
- internal branding;
- presentation skills;
- creativity.

When asked what skills and knowledge they needed to develop further their credibility and effectiveness, respondents included:

- influencing and negotiation;
- organizational change/change management;
- psychology of communication;
- organizational development;
- understanding the business;
- training, coaching, consulting;
- leadership communication and behaviour;
- process/best practice;
- political skills.

The researchers, however, were concerned at the lack of emphasis on measurement and business awareness. They felt the skills needed should also include these elements missing from the respondents' lists:

- strategic thinking ability;
- business awareness/literacy;
- writing and presentation skills;
- branding;
- e-communication development;
- creative communication skills;
- facilitation skills;
- consultancy skills;
- staying power and self-belief.

On the learning front, most respondents were not impressed by the formal education on offer, and conferences were not regarded particularly favourably.

Practitioners seem to rely on a range of organizations operating in the sector: the International Association of Business Communicators, British Association of Communicators in Business and the Communication Directors Forum in addition to the Internal Communication Alliance.

Although everyone feels that communication is something required of all managers, the reality in terms of what is delivered on a day-to-day basis is rather different. Internal communication needs to be planned, coordinated and linked to business strategy, and this is where the specialist fits in.

The respondents feel the role has value by providing insights into the internal stakeholder. Well managed and targeted internal communication activity can help employees understand their company and its direction. Internal communicators working with other specialists can help gain employee commitment to the success of the organization.

In times of change the role has a major part to play in convincing stakeholders of the need for change, especially when it can mean great uncertainty. The role can act as a safety valve in creating a point for listening to employees and enabling their views to be heard.

It should lead the information flow and advise the chief executive on the style, timing, targeting and content of communication. It provides a coaching role to managers, equipping them with the skills to communicate more professionally with their teams.

'Companies underestimate the power of internal communication at their peril. Not only can it create a better relationship between employer and employee, it can have a significant impact on the way employees behave and perform and therefore the way that a business performs', according to the report's author.

HOW OTHERS SEE IT

Honesty and integrity come up time and time again as important not just for the practitioner but also for the top teams of the organizations in which the communicator operates. Without the commitment of the top team the function will not have the credibility it needs.

Having the confidence to stand up to management and argue a case that runs counter to whatever it is they are voicing or expecting is as important and as difficult for the internal communicator as it is for the externally focused practitioner. Credibility is also helped by total competence – a thorough grasp of the situation, clear writing, respect for deadlines and budgets, and sensitivity to commercial issues are all needed.

Tom Harvey, Head of Communications at Nationwide, believes 'you have to have a healthy degree of scepticism. No matter where you go there will still be someone to overclaim, you have to have the objectivity to look at it and to challenge it from the staff perspective. You have to go through the puff sometimes generated by colleagues driven with an over enthusiasm for their own specialism and to distil that that is different.'

His background is advertising: 'Advertising does entail dismantling a particular case put by a manufacturer to arrive at the benefit for the end audience. I find that very helpful.'

Jeremy Redhouse of consultants Redhouse Lane also feels internal communication may well require competencies more commonly found in advertising than public relations. He also believes that communicators need a large degree of information technology experience and feels the battle between IT and communications for the natural home of the intranet is not quite over yet.

According to Justine Guest at Trinity Management Communications, 'a higher proportion of leaders in companies recognise the specialist skills and knowledge required to talk with the media, whereas most people think they know how to do internal communications'.

The internal adviser becomes much more 'the coach, the facilitator, the nurturer of people and their communications skills. Influencing and coaching skills need to be finely tuned.' The need for such skills is not as evident in public relations roles as it is for internal roles – she argues that the approach to internal and external communications is different.

With face-to-face communication the favourite medium certainly of the recipient, dialogue is coming under particular scrutiny. This is an area not always particularly well exploited by the corporate communications or human resources functions.

A head for figures could also help – not just those that the department produces but the spreadsheets that indicate the health of the organization. Such knowledge will also secure the confidence of those in the boardroom.

In conclusion, perhaps the most important thing to remember is that communication is not, and should not be, about what the board of directors does to employees. It is very much a two-way or even multi-directional process as future chapters will demonstrate.

Very little has been said about the importance of keeping a close watch on what is going on in the external world. There is a danger that an internal communicator focused entirely on the company's internal world will miss what the external media is saying about the company. Your employees read the local and national newspapers and other publications and will be affected by what they read. It is important for the internal communicator to work closely with external relations colleagues to ensure messages are consistent. Hopefully the internal communicator will also be better prepared to spot trouble on the horizon.

KEY POINTS TO REMEMBER

- Credibility is essential.
- Internal communication often plays second fiddle to external communication in the boardroom.
- Internal communicators need to build business skills as well as their specialist knowledge and skills.
- An advisory or coaching role is increasing in importance.
- Communicators need diplomacy, listening skills and tenacity.
- They need to understand and interpret spreadsheets and budgets.

3

Your audience – who are they?

Your communications programme has one fundamental requirement. It must align your communications objectives with those of the organization.

So how do you identify and segment your targets? That could and should be rather more complex than a media relations programme. Jeremy Redhouse, Managing Director of communications consultancy Redhouse Lane, says internal communication requires greater sensitivity towards the audience and a deep understanding of the organization. He believes the skills may be more akin to the advertising focus on the product and the client. 'You have got to be careful not to patronise them or go over their heads.'

Take some time to look at those groups in terms of where they are positioned in the organization. Then you can start to plan how to reach them and what tools to use.

FRONT-LINE STAFF

These are employees with most contact with the customer. They are often the least considered group but the one with the greatest potential for impact

– good or ill – on your external customers and by extension your organization's performance on a day-to-day basis.

Today's front-line staff could be literally facing the customer on the supermarket checkout, but are just as likely to be based unseen in call centres or in production in what is left of the country's industrial base. Some could even be individuals working from home. Depending on the nature of the work, they could be highly trained and qualified individuals, or have left school with few formal qualifications.

Employees working in factories may also not get close to a computer screen, so at BMW Hams Hall, the assembly areas for manufacturing-based employees sport 52-inch flat screens with touch-screen interactive capability.

The AA patrol force, the company's front-line operation, do not meet up with each other as a team other than that at diaried team meetings. These individuals need to be kept informed not just of company developments but also of advances in their industry, to keep their skills up to date when providing help to the AA's member base. A good mix of media including print and also videos and audio cassettes supplemented by face-to-face meetings with line managers keeps them involved. Eventually much more will be delivered via new laptop computer equipment in the cab.

At IBM, employees naturally have access to the latest in technology but have to be motivated to use it to the best effect. Use of text messaging ensures they are kept informed of company results or breaking news more fully displayed on other media.

Pharmaceutical company Smith & Nephew Medical (wound care) has a globally spread salesforce. Some have intranet access, some not. Audio cassettes are a major part of the communication mix and enable potentially wasted hours to be put to profitable use.

At Capital One Bank in Nottingham, half the staff work in a call centre. Rather than sending out an e-mail to announce a new system, the 'messengers' get dressed up and carry the message around the building. But the intranet is used for news, backed up by face-to-face briefings with managers, newsletters and the occasional video.

SUPERVISORS/LINE MANAGERS

It is something of a given in internal communication circles that front-line staff place greater value on information related to their personal work needs delivered to them by their line managers or supervisors. Surveys of staff attitudes also show workers prefer to hear the good and the bad news from those that have day-to-day supervision of their workload.

There are still some organizations where a briefing is more than likely to be a rallying cry from a latter-day Attila the Hun with a top-down approach.

This is possibly the result of a failure to recognize that communication and presentation skills are not necessarily natural gifts bestowed on all.

Line managers may need to be supported in what to them may be a new role – communication. Chapter 14 describes how a number of organizations have approached upskilling their own people to communicate with staff. This provides the internal communication specialist with the opportunity to shake off the shackles of delivery mode and become more of a facilitator for the line manager.

SENIOR MANAGEMENT/MIDDLE MANAGEMENT

This group refers to the layer or layers between the front-line management and board level. Middle management has been included, although points in the previous section can also be applied to this level as there is always some overlap.

As these individuals are unlikely to be enjoying day-to-day contact with customers, or what has been termed 'customer-facing staff', they could be seen to be out of touch with both these critical groups. Senior and middle management can be seen as an audience in their own right, or again as an important agent in the delivery of communication to other parts of the organization.

Middle managers are often perceived as a block, and where a lot of communication gets stuck. Justine Guest of Trinity Management Communications suggests that, with middle managers, part of the trick is to engage them directly and not just tell them. Often a higher proportion of time and effort is spent engaging the most senior managers: 'But respecting middle managers is important as they often have the large-scale jobs managing significant numbers of staff – their impact particularly on areas such as customer service is crucial.' She says: 'Managers tend to be promoted because they have knowledge and expertise in the business and not necessarily because they are good at communicating. Managers need to be effective communicators, an e-mail will simply not suffice.'

BOARD/DIRECTOR

A recent survey showed that where the CEO really believes in internal communications, the scope for that internal communications team is far in excess of what it would otherwise be. It is not just about money or budget: if the CEO is behind it, the standard is set for other leaders to follow.

Board directors are often regarded as the external mouthpiece and visible leaders and role models of the organization. It is the role of the communication specialist to advise these 'mouthpieces', which takes a certain degree of confidence unlikely to be found in new entrants to the function.

Speaking at a spring 2003 Internal Communication Alliance meeting, Patrick Dunne of 3i said the chair and chief executive of commercial organizations often undervalued internal communication and were themselves often unfocused. He suggested grabbing a few moments at unplanned, informal meetings including in the lift and the back of a cab, to bring some influence to bear.

VOLUNTARY SECTOR – TRUSTEES, VOLUNTEERS, MEMBERS

The not-for-profit sector encompasses registered charities and more generally organizations which do not have profit as the motivator. There are some distinct differences when this sector is compared with the public and commercial sectors. Boundaries are blurred between service users, paid staff and unpaid trustees and/or directors and volunteers. To confuse matters further many not-for-profit organizations have trading arms and in very many cases have dual status as a limited company to protect themselves.

Many of the 180,000 or so registered charities that exist do so without any paid employees at all, but as they develop they will end up with the typical mix of both paid and unpaid staff. Quite a few organizations have volunteers operating out of autonomous regional groups and in some cases service users can also be volunteers, staff or trustees.

Tailoring communication for any combination of these very different audiences is a major challenge. Add to that the usual chronic lack of funding, and the scale of the task positively overawes. This sector makes a virtue out of gaining extra mileage from all its communications.

AT ONE REMOVE

With many public sector organizations having contracted out activity to outside companies and in some cases charities, the person sitting at a desk may not feel their first loyalty is to your organization but to the one that is subcontracted to deliver that activity.

Vertex, for example, now runs no fewer than 67 services for Westminster City Council including emergency services, libraries and parking. Staff were transferred across from the council but the group also recruited new staff, bringing the staff group to some 300. In addition, the company works in partnership with other contractors. Audiences for internal communication can also include the staff representing the client side (the council). A particular emphasis on clear information but also a very delicate hand is required as staff are phased in from one organization to the other over time.

Partner organizations are working ever more closely together and it may become necessary to get to grips with different approaches and attitudes. Public sector organizations often work across agencies to deliver services to particular client groups these days. Learning disability will bring together specialists working in health, social services and education, and all these can be working for different agencies – the health service or local authority in this case.

The mix is complicated still further by the inclusion of different disciplines and professions to which staff may feel they hold the greater loyalty. So hard is it to get these various factions to work together that at least one charity was brought into existence to effectively encourage greater cooperative working. As the way services are delivered changes, often according to the whims of politicians at local as well as national level, internal communicators may find themselves having to design communications programmes accordingly.

CREATIVES AND SPECIALISTS

Communicators face similar dilemmas when designing communication programmes which will meet the often demanding requirements of creatives and other highly qualified staff as well as a more general audience.

When Chandler Gooding devised a new publication to unite the disparate parts of Sky TV, they found they had inadvertently alienated the technicians who install the systems. They had previously been left out of the picture provided by a number of different publications, but the unifying magazine which was produced was not technical enough for them. The swift addition of a more appropriate publication just for this group did the trick.

Public relations consultancies can eventually grow to a size requiring a more structured approach to their own internal communication needs. Creatives will wish to be addressed rather differently from account handling staff. Lawyers are again a challenging audience to satisfy. So are PhD-loaded scientists.

Creatives and other specialists are often interested in the latest innovation and will also respond to a novel approach to a subject matter. Their backgrounds will often be very different from, say, the accounts or human resources departments. It is important not to talk down to them, especially when talking about their specific fields, but it is also vital not to make assumptions about their knowledge of areas alien to them.

DIVERSITY

This effectively covers every aspect of an individual's own identity that may have to be considered when delivering communication programmes.

It is often overlooked that different geographical cultures have different approaches to working practice. In an article entitled 'Teamwork is easier to agree than to do' published in the *Daily Telegraph*, 25 May 2000, Brian Bloch points out that the team approach is in fact an Eastern orientation and that in the West we prefer to concentrate on individual effort.

Keeping track on what motivates this year's graduates is another complication to be considered. Capital One Bank staff are relatively youthful in outlook which may explain the preference for dressing up to cheerlead staff through announcements.

Organizations like BUPA have a strong weighting towards women so it is unlikely that there would be a great deal of coverage of male-orientated subjects in their regular publications. However, coming generations might be different: apparently football is a favoured sport among members of Girlguiding UK.

Threats to pensions mean that workforces could well be getting older, and legislation to penalize discriminatory practices may well assist in putting the grey hairs back into the workplace. Assumptions are often made that older staff may prefer not to receive the bulk of their communication by e-mail and intranet.

In conclusion, putting your target audience under a microscope for close inspection, and investing in research to find out what they want to know and how they would prefer it to be presented, is a vital early step in the communication process.

SEGMENTATION – THE WAY AHEAD

External communicators, especially those with a grounding in marketing and advertising, will be familiar with the need to segment audiences. This chapter has concentrated on particular levels of the organization in which a section of the audience may be located. We have looked very briefly at the particular differences to be found in the voluntary sector by way of paid and unpaid staff and management.

Chapter 8 will concentrate on the selection of communication channels, vehicles and activities available which differently sized organizations may favour in different sectors and at different stages of their development.

But in addition to establishing where your targets are situated, it is worthwhile to consider what else may impact on effective communication.

Anti-discriminatory legislation will mean that in many cases in future a more diverse audience will present itself. You will need to take account of the qualifications that these people will possess as well as considering the sector in which you operate.

A quick spot of desktop research using your organization's own records (while taking account of data protection legislation) should establish a framework within which you can then operate. A preponderance of younger males in their first jobs (advertising sales representatives spring to mind) would require a very different approach than perhaps a more widely dispersed older workforce (vehicle maintenance workers based out of the office).

WAYS TO SEGMENT YOUR INTERNAL AUDIENCE

- age;
- gender;
- ethnic background;
- location;
- educational qualifications;
- part time/full time;
- payroll or not;
- on site/off site;
- time with organization;
- position in organization.

Many of the theoretical models you might apply to meet their communications needs are explored in the next chapter.

KEY POINTS TO REMEMBER

- Front-line staff prefer to hear the news straight from line managers.
- A mix of media (intranet, publications, audio/visual) will best serve hard-to-reach groups.
- Middle managers should be seen as facilitators rather than blockages.
- Communication and communicators need the backing of the CEO.
- Creatives and specialists should be handled sensitively.
- Take account of diversity (age, gender, race, culture, etc).

4

Theories into practice

Very few of the many internal communicators involved in the production of this book even casually referred to the 'T' word. Theory, certainly as it relates to communication, did not appear on the radar until purposefully put there by the author.

Perhaps there is no time in the average jam-packed working day for the in-house communicator to even think about communication theory let alone begin to apply it to existing practice, or even better use it as a framework or aid to help shape their future plans and activities.

Different professional and educational backgrounds could also have a part to play. Professionals encountered in both in-house and consultancy settings come from a range of disciplines, perhaps emphasizing a point made in Nick Helsby's 2002 report, *The Rise of the Internal Communicator*, that few volunteer internal communication as having been their initial career of choice. They had studied enormously varied subjects ranging from comparative religion to structural engineering, but there were more familiar topics along the way such as English. Interestingly media studies was not mentioned.

This chapter is intended as something of a smorgasbord of theories that could provide insights into organizational and management behaviour and programmes, and could also provide the ammunition to improve either in imaginative hands. Most pop up somewhere at a relevant Masters degree level but do not appear to be common knowledge among all internal communicators.

The selection is also intended to reflect the nature of the discipline which is seen not only to encompass the public relations/marketing end of the spectrum but also runs through to human resources and change management.

Many of the communications models and schools of thought which can be brought to bear on internal communication overlap and it is especially difficult to sort them into neat camps. This chapter first takes a detour through the field of organizational culture; this provides the context for looking first at process theory as set against the semiotics school. Aspects of individual and mass communications theory will also be explored. The final section will look at computer-mediated communication which can be regarded as criss-crossing all and is a growing field of study in itself.

THE FOUR CULTURES OF THE ORGANIZATION

In the current world of the internal communicator there is the dawning realization that the old traditional hierarchical form of organization communication – top down – is still very much a reality. In the early 21st century a distressing number of organizations seem to be retreating from a more collaborative approach to communication back to at least some degree of centralized control.

To gain an understanding of what really makes organizations tick you can do no better than turn to the classic in the field, Charles Handy's *Understanding Organizations* (1985). First published in 1976 it still has a lot to say on the reality of organizations.

Handy is particularly insightful on power and influence, although his pragmatic approach and way of expressing what makes them what they are may not sit that comfortably in today's lexicon. Handy has identified four types of culture that reflect the way those leading organizations prefer things to be.

Power culture

Small entrepreneurial organizations are likely to have a power culture centred on the founder. In this model the founder is often the voice of the organization and will, at least in its early days, take control of communications. At a later stage professional communicators might be appointed but the founder will remain a prominent factor in both internal and external relations. Figure 4.1 illustrates this culture.

Figure 4.1 *Power culture – type of organizational culture most commonly found in organizations run by entrepreneurs* (Charles Handy)

Role culture

Bureaucracy has been something of a term of abuse for many years. It was certainly recognized as such when Handy was writing his volume 20 years ago. So in order to move on from those connotations he has used the term 'role'.

The role organization places its emphasis on function and specialism. It has many procedures and rules. Job descriptions are prevalent here as are procedures for doing things and rules for settling disputes.

In these organizations the post is likely to be more important than the postholder and, conversely, the postholder gains their credibility from the position they hold. These organizations are likely to have been around for some time and operate where economies of scale are important. They can also be slow to change and in reacting to shifts in market forces.

More positively, there is a clear hierarchy, providing a means of appointing, promoting and rewarding staff on merit. Large companies and public sector bodies in particular might not want to see themselves as bureaucracies, but it is likely they retain some elements of this kind of organizational culture.

Large organizations will have the economies of scale to be able to invest time and resources to ensure their messages are consistently and constantly communicated. They are more likely to invest in multiple media to achieve this. In the research for this book there were no examples of organizations of this size relying on simply one channel of communication.

This type of organization will have at least one if not a team of communicators. There are often multiple routes to get things done, but equally, layers of bureaucracy will often result in complex approval systems which can stifle creativity and stall response times. Figure 4.2 illustrates this culture.

Person culture

Within some bureaucracies can reside traces of yet another culture which can thrive quite happily within but have little affiliation to the whole. Educational establishments and hospitals particularly spring to mind.

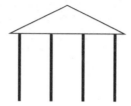

Figure 4.2 *Role culture – type of organizational culture typified by bureaucratic organizations based on heavily defined structure and procedure* (Charles Handy)

Handy himself also cites barristers' chambers, architects' practices and small consultancies as having their focus on the person culture. This may sound rather like the power culture prevalent in entrepreneurial organizations but is in fact quite different.

Here the focus, if it can be described as such, is on the individuals themselves as separate individuals who choose to work together. Where this kind of group has sprung up within universities and healthcare settings there can be real stresses and strains with the overarching structure, which will often be largely bureaucratic.

Concentrations of highly skilled professionals are less likely to pay attention to messages they perceive as having been centrally generated by the organization. They are more likely to be focused on their individual professions and will look outside the wider organization to their professional institutions for their information needs. A deep understanding of the allegiances these individuals hold will assist the corporately based communicator to begin to win their trust.

One way to build the communicator's credibility with this kind of group is to enlist its members as specialist advisers and use their expertise when fine-tuning communications efforts. (See Chapter 15 for tips on how to build editorial advisory panels.) Figure 4.3 illustrates this culture.

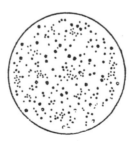

Figure 4.3 *Person culture – type of organizational culture most commonly found where organizations exist to support the individuals working there; partnerships in particular* (Charles Handy)

Task culture

A fourth culture which is likely to be more familiar in today's working climate than the days in which Handy first wrote his classic is the task culture. This is focused on the job in hand or the project. It is also likely to be a feature in organizations with dispersed operations, although the larger the organization the more likely it will share characteristics more akin to the role or person cultures. Communicating with geographically dispersed publics along with other hard-to-reach groups is covered in Chapters 12 and 11 respectively.

The task- or project-orientated culture may be by its very nature nimble on its feet and able to form and re-form depending on the requirements of the task in hand, but it does have its limitations. It is unlikely that you would be able to run a large complex organization along these lines for very long – there are no economies of scale and the constituent parts have no long-term experience of working together. But for a major one-off activity, project groups based on the task culture will do the job very well.

For the internal communicator this kind of culture will provide fertile ground in terms of material for publication or broadcast. The downside is that where the efforts of the group are concentrated on one task there will be little chance to expand on initiatives. Communication efforts may well deal simply with the task in hand, offering little promise of continuity or development. In the geographically dispersed organization the audiences are likely to be fragmented and so more focused solely on their section of the picture. Figure 4.4 illustrates this culture.

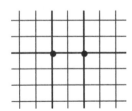

Figure 4.4 *Task culture – type of organizational culture found where culture is focused on the project and ad hoc teams are created and disbanded frequently* (Charles Handy)

Many communication consultancies include culture change or what is now termed 'change management' within their services to help organizations identify and manage employees through the main areas of business, cultural and behavioural change.

These are, firstly, the large organizational infrastructure shifts created by strategic business change, eg merger and acquisition, which often include job losses. Secondly, issues management: to help protect and/or enhance the brand or corporate reputation here it is essential to align both internal and external messages. Thirdly, on a more positive note, engaging and energizing employees behind the business goals is vital.

There could be three approaches: the bald statement ('like it or lump it'); invited comments on stated options (when a decision has already been made behind the scenes); or genuine choice and participation. The problem arises when the communication and approaches are muddled, and 'no choice' is in fact dressed up as an invitation to choose.

PROCESS THIS WAY OR GIVE US A SIGN

John Fiske's *Introduction to Communication Studies* (1992) is essential reading for anyone wishing to unravel the process and semiotics models of communication. According to him the process school concentrates on the 'transmission of messages' and how accurately the chosen system of moving messages around actually works.

This model owes a lot to early models which had been devised during the Second World War to investigate mechanical methods of sending signals. Having moved out of the telegraph office or radio room, proponents have drawn heavily on social sciences, psychology and sociology. The process school could be argued to fit most neatly into the role culture model.

The second school, semiotics, instead focuses attention on the 'production and exchange of meanings' and looks at the interplay between people and 'texts' (this can mean images and artefacts as well as words) which result in the creation of meaning. This school focuses on semiotics – the science of signs and meanings – and concentrates on linguistics. It is likely to have more to offer the power, task and possibly person cultures.

Returning to the process school, despite its mechanistic approach it is widely recognized as having set the scene for the development of the entire Communication Studies movement. The mathematical theory of communication came from US wartime studies at Bell Telephone and emphasized the channels of communication that at the time were telephone and radio.

Published in 1949, the Shannon and Weaver model was intended to overcome the difficulty in sending a large amount of information through one channel. It also sought to measure how much information one channel could carry. An engineer himself, Shannon was actually looking at how to send electrical impulses most efficiently from one place to another but felt this mechanistic approach could apply to human interaction.

Resembling little more than a line linking a series of boxes en route from source to receiver, the model did, however, take some limited account of interference. Originally designed to tackle technical problems, it was then expanded to look at how well meaning was carried. The belief was that provided the message was properly encoded or stated, it should be received as sent. The authors also felt that the model could also be used to measure the effect of the message on the conduct of the receiver. This last factor has laid the model open to charges of propaganda.

The starting point – the source of the information – is regarded as the decision maker, the transmitter is self-explanatory and the information becomes the signal despatched via the channel to the receiver.

Shannon and Weaver took account of the notion of redundancy; this refers to built-in extra or duplicated information which enables the message to get through to its destination. Passing the time of day and repeating a telephone number may seem pointless, but this checking and rechecking is a demonstration of the use for redundancy. Later models by other researchers added concepts such as feedback.

A linear approach also becomes apparent in many more recent communications models, most especially the hypodermic needle approach. Here messages are simply injected into the recipient who, it is assumed, will accept them without argument and without distorting the incoming data.

Phillip Clampitt (1991) in his book *Communicating for Managerial Effectiveness* provides a more violent analogy to the needle, preferring the arrow approach. This remains essentially the one-way, linear approach.

The arrow model describes an information source sending a message via the transmitter through a channel to its destination. This first model did not recognize that the receiver might wish to give feedback, as it was essentially a passive model. Its only advantage was that it encouraged the sender to think clearly through the message they wished to transmit.

When applied to social communication the linear model did not quite fit so gave way to the more triangular approach adopted by Newcomb and others. They built in extra components to recognize that the recipient might bring his or her thought processes to bear on the contents of the message and give a response. Some rather complicated diagrams result.

The two-way element recognized in these marginally more sophisticated models is described as the circuit approach by Clampitt. There is still something of a mechanistic flavour apparent. Whereas Clampitt's arrow manager 'targets his audience', the circuit manager is 'going with the flow' and 'making connections'.

GOLDEN OLDIE REVISITED

So might the process school approach to communication be alive and well in the 21st century? Although the term is not used, it is obvious from the comments of independent communication consultant Richard Gaunt that it still remains an influence for some managers.

In his management-focused approach he asserts that key ingredients for success include clear objectives and measurement criteria, and understanding of the strategy and agenda of both top management and of other levels. But he argues language and context should be that of the receiver not the sender, and that media used should be quick, accessible and understandable with little jargon. This places the emphasis on face-to-face communication.

Repetition, regularity and consistency are key and this is where the notion of 'redundancy' springs to mind. Most importantly, however, Gaunt says the audience should be treated as customers, 'not mindless battery hens', and that the communicator should talk about more than just the successes.

Frequently for managements, information and communication can be confused as one and the same thing. Information is not necessarily processed at the receiving end; despatch does not automatically lead to results. Those on the receiving end may complain of overload but still perceive themselves as never receiving sufficient communication.

Postman or business partner?

So is the internal communicator a postman or a business partner? The way managements respond to this question can determine whether or not communicators are seen simply as a means to shift chunks of data from one end of the organization to another. Technology has only served to increase the likelihood that management will assume the production of spreadsheets and bullet point-style presentations constitutes good communication.

Not as much has changed as might have been wished for according to Roger D'Aprix, who devised a communication model more than 20 years ago in his book *Communicating for Productivity*. His theory is revisited in an interview with him conducted by B Gorman writing in *Strategic Communication Management* (2003). The original 1982 model argued that employee communication should be regarded as a strategic process. This formed the basis for employee engagement for years to come, but Gorman asked if it would remain relevant in light of the way the world of work has changed.

The model looked at workplace communication from the employees' point of view and asked what they wanted and needed to perform well and to be satisfied. It focused in particular on exchanges between managers and employees. D'Aprix's model looked at job responsibilities, feedback on performance, individual needs, work unit objectives and results, the values and direction of the organization and empowerment or scope for the employee. All of these could be seen to sit well with Maslow's theories of a hierarchy of needs explained later in this chapter.

In pondering the major changes in the world since the model was created, D'Aprix said there had been additional complications. He argued that today's internal communicator now has to take account of globalization, increasing demands from shareholders and security analysts, the end of the social contract, the devaluing of employees and their contribution to the bottom line, and the explosion of technology.

Research carried out by BrandEnergy Research (Hutton) on behalf of the Chartered Institute of Public Relations in 2004 and published in *Profile* magazine suggests that senior communications practitioners certainly make the mental link between effective internal communication and a healthy organization.

Those most impressed by their organization's internal communications were more likely to feel that their workforces were encouraged to express their views, that the function was well integrated with other organizational functions, and that there was a good match with external communications.

These views are backed by D'Aprix who believes that managers who take the time to communicate with employees ultimately save time: 'The effective organization is still the one that recognises that it must build a community of like-minded people who are on the same page, moving in the same direction, motivated by working together and who have a sense of being connected together in a worthwhile enterprise. That is what gives meaning to work and even to human existence.'

SEMIOTICS – READING THE SIGNS

There are no clear-cut lines between the process and semiotics schools. This is demonstrated by Jakobson, a linguist working in the 1960s: his model manages to span both. He uses the familiar linear model but adds in the concept of code which refers to a shared system of meaning shifting the emphasis away from the sender. He moves closer to the more modern notion of communication being the creation of many rather than just one person.

The semiotics school uses a very different language from that of the process-driven model. Here terms like 'sign', 'denotation' and 'connotation' are used with the emphasis on how an individual generates meaning from what are simply a series of strokes on a piece of paper. The word is a symbol rather than a carrier of meaning, so the letters CAT can mean more than just a four-legged animal depending on its context.

A strength of the semiotics school is that it captures elements not included in the process model such as the impact of gestures and other non-verbal communication on how the spoken word is actually interpreted. Very little attention is paid to the words spoken in an exchange, as opposed to the accompanying gestures.

Semiotics is potentially much more fruitful territory for the creative communicator wanting to make effective use of imagery and language rather than focusing on the more technical aspects of transmission.

The next section turns the spotlight on mass communication research. Its application to this field underlines the view that the audience can be pretty determined to read things its own way.

FOCUS ON THE MASS OR THE INDIVIDUAL

Few of us can be unaware of the products of the mass media, whether employer or employee. Many publications produced for an internal readership are created to look like the magazines and newspapers available on the high street, while video programmes often look like mainstream broadcasting. Intranets resemble their external counterparts in the web world. The mass media approach is likely to be most in evidence in bureaucratic organizations as they have the resources to sustain it.

Around the time that Shannon and Weaver were working on their process model, Lasswell was producing a model which could be used more specifically for mass communication. It looked at who said what, through which channel, to whom and with what result. As Fiske (1992) points out, the model is still linear in appearance, as in fact is most mass communication research, and Westley and MacLean modified Lasswell's model in 1957 and effectively introduced the editorial or gatekeeper role, a vital concept in both internal and external communication.

Windahl, Signitzer and Olson (1993) introduce the intriguing concept of the obstinate audience. They state that the mass communication audience does not always accept what it is spoon-fed by the media. Perhaps this is just as true of the organizational communication version as it is of the news-stands. Windahl and colleagues also unpick the notion of audiences as passive receptacles and quote a range of research which shows audiences taking a much more active role in making sense of what they consume in terms of media.

There is a veritable treasure trove of theories from mass communication which can be brought to bear on internal communications. Windahl *et al* talk in particular about uses and gratifications, and other theories of interest include agenda setting, spiral of silence and knowledge gap theories which are explained briefly below.

Uses and gratifications suggests that the audience actively consumes their chosen media, often using it in unanticipated ways. Selection of channel may also relate to issues around age, social class and even income. McQuail (1992) lists basic uses as seeking information, reinforcing personal values, finding out about others and sheer entertainment.

Agenda setting argues the media works by suggesting the subjects that individuals should be thinking about. Brosius and Wermann (1996) question who sets the agenda. They argue that it is a two step-flow process recognizing mediation and shifting influence between media and public. This model also takes account of the roles of gatekeepers and opinion formers which can be applied equally to internal and external audiences. In internal communication it is essential to identify those among the target group who allow access to the wider group and who operate in the gatekeeping or champion role. They might also be the trailblazers and are respected as sources of information and so are seen as undertaking the opinion-former role. Equally they could act as blocking mechanisms.

Other theories of particular interest more usually applied to the mass media perspective include the spiral of silence which links with the knowledge gap theory. In the first theory, individuals do not admit ignorance and stay silent, often due to what they perceive as peer pressure. Silence does not therefore mean understanding. Knowledge gap applies where an informed minority is able to gain more information than the rest. This could skew surveys into take-up of knowledge if the sample is not comprehensive enough to unearth those not in the know.

O'Sullivan *et al* (1992) refer to preferred and deviant readings, and separately elaborated and restricted codes. Relating these to internal communication channels, preferred readings would be the official organizational or management material, while the workforce having conducted a deviant reading may come to different conclusions.

Elaborated and restricted codes relate to the type of language used. The former might be used by the better educated, whereas the latter might be used by the less well-informed who would therefore feel shut out by the use of profession- or organization-specific jargon. This would be apparent in a hospital setting where doctors might have very different ways of describing health conditions from, say, porters or administrative staff.

THE INDIVIDUAL REVISITED

Although, like most of those interviewed for this book, she did not identify known models of communication theory, Caroline Bramley, Head of Internal Communications Services at communications consultancy Flag, is probably taking a view in favour of the individual rather than the system when she declares: 'People have seen through the management consultancy use of models. People are not processes, people are unpredictable, rational, emotional and this cannot be captured in a model.'

Psychology provides perspectives centred on the individual. From this science comes Maslow's theory of self-actualization which is rooted in his hierarchy of needs model. This is more usually applied to external customers but works just as well for internal audiences.

Figure 4.5 *Maslow's hierarchy of needs – the individual's progression of needs and wants*

A pyramid is used to demonstrate the rising hierarchy of needs starting with physiological needs (food, etc); safety; belonging; self-esteem or success; and finally, self-actualization or development to full personal capacity. See Figure 4.5.

All other needs would usually have to have been satisfied before the individual arrives at the pinnacle of self-actualization. These 'needs' might be applied differently to different staff groups. It is likely that the shop-floor worker will be more closely focused on the first two or three layers of the pyramid if they are at the earlier stages of their career than, say, the managing director. But do not jump to easy conclusions, as other factors might be playing a part including educational status. Security is unlikely to be such an issue for a graduate high-flier on the first rungs of the corporate ladder. Taking time to understand the motivations of individuals rather than treating them as an amorphous group should pay dividends for the internal communicator.

In writing about consumer rather than employee behaviour, Williams (1989) refers to the 'black box' model where the individual is seen to respond to an externally applied stimulus. He uses as illustration the famous experiments with Pavlov's dogs and Skinner's rats which elicited response through reward and punishment. This could be likened to the carrot and stick management approach, where the carrot is the incentive and the stick rather speaks for itself.

Neurolinguistic programming is a more recent addition to the communications toolbox. It seeks to provide an explanation for individual preferences for processing information. Giving someone with a preference for pictures great slabs of text may not be the way to achieve great success with your programme.

Jonne Ceserani, of Synectics Europe, has suggested the brain does not simply hear the words of a speaker: at the same time it will be creating mental maps which serve to make sense of daily experiences. Imagery can mean very different things to different people, and for that matter to different cultures. To talk about 'killing a sacred cow' or 'white elephants' would offend some cultures. Choose your words wisely.

Returning to the psychological approach, Richard Varey (1997) draws attention to the early work produced by Eric Berne around transactional analysis. Here, how people relate to each other can be seen as role-playing, taking their cues from the way the family acts out various characteristics.

The roles of parent, adult and child can be seen to have both positive and negative aspects. A 'parent' may be positively supportive but more negatively be seen as controlling, while a 'child' could be playful and imaginative or disruptive. The ideal third way is the 'adult' approach, which is seen as the reasoned, logical approach. For effective communication to take place, both sides need to approach each other in a reasoned or adult way.

Rather a lot of the theories named by management writers in the past decade or so can seem, with the benefit of a backward glance, an older theory dressed up. For instance, when emotional intelligence which focuses on human relationships seemed at the end of its natural life, up popped the notion of the spiritual quotient. This promised to delve deeper into the individual's soul.

Theories do not quite have the short shelf-life of high street fashion, but like all sartorial golden oldies they can have their day in the sun once again with a brand new tag. In the run-up to the second Gulf War, publications like *Management Today* were heralding the return of the macho boss with such niceties as people-centred skills being given short shrift.

SHALL WE DANCE? THE COOPERATIVE MODEL

Most of these models appear focused on the individual. For Clampitt (1991) there is a way forward in his theory of 'communication as dance'. This model has shifted from the 'results'-driven arrow and 'understanding'-motivated circuit models previously described. His more individualistic approach seeks out the coordination of meanings with both parties adjusting their communications in response to the responses they receive. They do not have to agree, as this model takes into account the fact that people may have different interpretations.

The example of such a coordinated conversation Clampitt uses in his book ends with the employee telling his manager to clear off after a series of playful insults have been directed at the employee. So it is not clear whether this model is included as recognition of the reality of everyday communication or as the model we should be striving for. Could make for some fun exchanges!

An extension of Clampitt's dance motif, in that it is purposefully designed to emphasize the positive and is focused on the individual, is the appreciative inquiry approach. Management consultancy Questions of Difference (QoD) has used this approach with a range of clients. Working in small groups, individuals are encouraged to learn from what has worked well for them in the past and use this to develop approaches to apply to other areas of their working lives. The individual to be coached identifies individuals from their peers, the people they manage and those who manage them to pinpoint the successful behaviours which can be further developed.

The supporting players in the endeavour are in turn developed as individuals, which should serve to develop the organization's skills as a whole.

QoD also has what it calls the TICing Model of Communication. TIC stands for 'Time, Internal, Context' and identifies 12 significant influences that may impact on how an individual will communicate in any given conversation or instance. Understanding these enables individuals to be more aware of how best to communicate with others and to interpret what is said in a given set of circumstances.

Conflict is seen as an expression of differences rather than something negative. Questioning is seen as a most powerful tool which will help people to change direction through curiosity. In 'reframing and hearing', individuals are helped to make sense of past events and responses and move away from blame to a cooperative approach.

QoD believes that organizational identity is predominantly formed through conversations and interactions between individuals, within teams and groups, and between management and staff.

COMPUTER-MEDIATED COMMUNICATION AND THE IMPLICATIONS

As a platform, the computer is affecting communication at every level. In some circles computer-mediated communication (CMC) is also referred to as 'electronic media' and covers intranet, group networks and websites. There is an increasingly large body of work on the implications of information technology on both organizations and society. So fast-moving is the area that papers published as little as five years ago look positively antique in their approach.

A welter of academic papers has generally looked at whether preferences for particular channels could be put down to organizational rank, whether electronic bulletin boards really link up that many people, and whether channels are providing a bridge between the interpersonal and the mass media.

One writer who almost begs to be included is the appropriately named Hacker (1996) who suggests CMC can empower politically. Hacker *et al* (1998) suggest that e-mail can increase organizational communication.

It is worth organizations taking account of the fact that e-mail can be used as an informal channel, a kind of thoroughly modern grapevine which could be transporting views quite alien to the company stance. Surveillance policies may defeat this in time.

Channels such as face-to-face communication are rated highly on what is termed the 'media richness gauge'. Those that remove the human interaction, including e-mail, are likely to settle further down the scale. Like the related concept of social presence, media richness is based on the premise that individuals prefer media offering direct human contact.

Reducing communication to 'byte-sized' chunks may have seemed the way that intranet and other computer-mediated communication channels were leading us. However, some believe the backlash has set in, with people now requiring all the context or background information that was previously jettisoned in favour of brevity.

D'Aprix (Gorman, 2003) also believes that relying on electronic rather than face-to-face communication with staff could have horrendous implications. He argues that e-mail is not well structured, and gives little opportunity for exchange of information. 'High touch' rather than 'high tech' is what is needed. Perhaps there is a role for the canny communicator to teach staff how to make appropriate use of the communications tools to hand and so regain the upper hand.

David Phillips (2001) sounds some further warning bells with concepts such as 'porosity' which he relates to the passage of information from within an organization to external audiences. Depending on the intention, this could be seen as the new millennium version of whistle blowing. Many such actions are just as likely to be as a result of pressing the wrong key, but the result could be the same – information going to the wrong place.

In Chapter 8 we explore computer-mediated communications such as websites, video conferencing and the like. It is important to emphasize that computer technology simply provides another platform for delivery. Choice of media should be based on whether the printed word, sound or visual elements are what is required to transmit the message most effectively. Otherwise we could be in danger of arriving back where it all began with the emphasis firmly on process rather than message.

KEY POINTS TO REMEMBER

- Identify the prevailing organizational culture – power, role, person or task.
- Look at current approaches to communication. Is it by exhortation, persuasion or discussion? So arrow, circuit or dance?
- Process or semiotics? Does your organization concentrate on the process of communication – the channels, vehicles? Or does it seek to generate common understanding (semiotics school)?
- Take lessons from the mass media. Look out for gatekeepers who can block as well as release information to a wider audience.
- Remember your audience is active and people may apply their own interpretations to your messages.
- Segment your audience according to life stage and culture as well as job.
- Do not get carried away with the latest technology – people still prefer the human touch in communication.

5

Managing internal communication in-house

THE BUSINESS CASE

In an ideal world internal communication should be a key responsibility for the chief executive of any organization whatever its size. The reality of course can be quite different.

It is most likely that the function will be delegated to a board director and through them to a particular department. Again we would all like to see that director being a communications or public relations specialist. But even if they are, they could come from a wide range of backgrounds. Structural engineers have been known to swap career horses rather successfully. All these factors can influence where the function ends up being slotted into the organization's structure. History, or the 'we've always done it this way' approach, may also dictate where internal communication will sit within an organization.

Internal communication is an imperative for even the smallest of organizations. It is arguably more difficult to manage a recalcitrant team of one, two or three than a much larger organization.

Having an in-house department, specialists or at the very least a dedicated person means the organization can be assured that those concerned will have experience of the organization and its culture. They, in theory, should have the required links with those who make decisions and also those who have the relevant information – not necessarily always the same people.

Trying to produce an internal publication – print or web-based – from outside the organization without insider knowledge can be a complete nightmare, at least in the early days of any contract. From the client side of the fence there might be concerns about confidentiality and a lack of confidence about the nature of the consultancy's other clients.

The choice between in-house department or external providers might also be determined by the size of the organization. A two- or even a 20-person band will have very different requirements from an international concern.

The BBC's head of the internal communication function Russell Grossman believes the most successful internal communication team is one with a diverse set of skills. These should include marketing, organizational development, journalism, public relations, change management and more. Diversity in terms of life stage is also important. Those making a life-long career of an organization will bring a different perspective from those passing through.

The dedicated team approach can, however, have its drawbacks in terms of commitment to the delivery of internal communication. Once someone has been made responsible for the function, it can be easy for other functions within the organization to wash their hands of any involvement. Creating an understanding of the reality of the function is essential in order to develop the sound working relationships necessary for delivering the goods.

Responsibility for internal communication should ultimately and ideally rest with the chief executive. Experts in the field believe commitment or the lack of it on the part of senior management and their willingness to devote time and resources to the internal communications function will determine its and the organization's success. Honesty and integrity at the upper corporate reaches will also help.

The best internal communications practitioners will fail if they do not have the support and commitment of the senior team, and they should ideally be part of it officially or unofficially.

WHO DOES IT

So having established that going in-house with the function is the preferred route for some, there are a number of places within the organization where the function might sit. What follows is intended to reflect what happens out in the field, but the solution most palatable to those from a public relations background will no doubt be one of the first two options. That is a dedicated internal communication department or a team with links to public relations or corporate communications and human resources.

A survey conducted among North American companies in the early 1990s showed a wide range of possibilities in terms of the departments in which internal communication could be housed. There were public affairs, corporate affairs/relations, human resources, finance, law, administration, advertising and marketing. In many of the UK examples included in this book, internal communications can be rubbing shoulders with an equally wide range.

Here are some options on where internal communication might sit within an organization.

Internal communication department

In an ideal world this would be every internal communicator's dream scenario – a dedicated department.

It is also possible that there could be mini-departments or individuals in dispersed organizations. This would look rather like a classic business organization structure with these far-flung teams reporting in to, or working in conjunction with, a central department and/or director.

The mining giant Rio Tinto runs its communication function very much along these lines. With over 250 locations worldwide it would be impossible to deliver anything bar the framework within which the communicators in the individual businesses operate. A country base varies from vast operations with thousands of employees to a lone geologist or two in the proverbial hole in the ground in some remote place.

A dedicated department allows other communications professionals in the organization to get on with what they do best – public affairs, media relations, community liaison.

There are some very exotic titles around – 'change management' crops up more than once. Barclaycard had a very large team of internal communicators brought together from a separate internal communication function and a change management team. This latter recognized the need for constant evolution in the business.

The wider Barclays group also recognizes change as the norm but divides its activities between internal and externally based teams according to the complexity of the programme.

'Performance and organization development' made an appearance in the local authority sector. What these intriguing names may be most indicative of is a desire to come up with a new label for the function.

There is a good argument for regarding the central communication function as facilitative rather than a delivery agent. Consultant Pamela Mounter asserts: 'Internal communications is the line management responsibility, the managers have to do it and the internal communications manager has to help manage it. If the board does not own it then you will not get anywhere.'

There is an inherent weakness in the stand-alone internal communications department. A dedicated internal communication team or specialist could become isolated. They may have finely honed skills in web design and publication production but they could be telling a slightly different story from those other professionals, especially if they have different line managers. External communicators could well be reporting to marketing while internal communicators could be overseen by human resources management.

An effective internal communication department needs to raise its credibility most especially inside the organization. Many outsiders, and quite a few insiders for that matter, do not understand that keeping a workforce informed can and should be as rewarding a job as carrying out essentially the same function with an external audience.

Good internal publications and websites are designed by people who recognize that those who read them are the same people looking at magazines, newspapers, websites and television programmes outside. The requirements for attractively laid out, well-researched information with a human twist does not change with the donning of the company uniform or the business suit.

A positive reason for having a dedicated internal communication team would be one of immediacy. They can roll into action as part of a crisis management team and if they have been allowed to do the job properly will have all the channels open and the communications vehicles ticking over and ready to go. Perhaps the best model is to see other departments as clients of the internal communications department.

Public relations/corporate communications

As we all know, the public relations, corporate communications, just plain communications, external affairs (or whatever) department can and ought to be the repository for communication knowledge. Those who see communication as a broad, essential part of management and organization direction will most probably favour internal communication sitting in or reporting to this function.

A survey of internal communication in local government by Paul Inglefield (2002) found more than half the respondents reported internal communications managed by corporate communications, but worryingly 14 per cent said it was not managed at all.

The downside of a non-dedicated team member will be that internal communication will get squeezed into the time left over from the competing demands of TV crews, external publication deadlines and the like. Those questioned in the local government survey appeared to be multi-talented and certainly multi-tasked individuals as they estimated they spent no more than a third of their time on the function.

A more positive aspect is that an internal communicator wearing an external hat will be able to keep messages to both audiences consistent. This would hopefully result in the kinds of credible publications, website, videos, etc that staff will want to read. It is also more likely that the PR professional will have the ear of senior management and the right level of credibility to ensure they can argue their case more successfully. If they have really been doing their job they will also have a wealth of externally originated material which will involve their internal publics in the same way as external audiences.

The PR practitioner should also bring an external focus to any problem areas, as how these issues are handled could have an impact on external perceptions. There is nothing like a juicy industrial tribunal case, particularly one involving sexual or racial harassment or discrimination, for destroying years of painstaking work in the organization and in the wider community.

Human resources

Human resources departments can be perceived as the mouthpiece of management. When there is bad news to be delivered on the job front it is most likely to be seen as coming from this department. They are also perceived, rightly or wrongly, as doing little more than administering diversity and equal opportunities programmes, wage-round negotiations, benefit packages, team and individual performance in the job, disciplinary procedures and the like.

However, an effective HR department would have early warning of relevant directives coming from Europe. Most particularly they would have taken account of the directive on employee consultation which is boosting demands on the internal communication function.

The HR team will have also been responsible for flagging up the effects of legislation designed to recognize the interests of employees from different cultural backgrounds and/or with disabilities. Specialists in the field could be well versed in communicating with a very diverse range of people – skills that the internal communication person would find useful in communicating more effectively.

The HR department or specialists within it are also likely to be involved in career development and staff training. Delivering those packages is unlikely to fall to the internal communication specialist or PR professional, but some communications input could improve the experience. These areas should also prove fruitful for material for publications and websites.

Marketing

A few years back the buzz phrase in marketing circles was 'internal marketing', and it seemed as if the marketing department had decided that internal communications should be part of its remit. After all, they could well be managing the sales team and much of that supervision would have required finely honed communication skills.

Although wider ranging than marketing, public relations is often seen as part of the marketing function, when marketing communication is at the fore, particularly in consumer or industrial sectors. This is rather like the view that public relations is just media relations – a common misconception.

Marketing has more of an external focus than human resources and is therefore more akin to the PR department. But again it could be argued that the focus is narrower than the PR function and is concentrated on the bottom line.

More positively, the internal communication practitioner would benefit from stronger links with the marketing function. Staff are interested in the results of campaigns and in new or renewed contracts – their livelihoods depend on them. Staff on the ground particularly in customer care centres need to know about the product, what it does and how it is being sold. Larger corporations are just as guilty as smaller ones of not equipping those in the firing line with the information needed to do their job.

Poor customer service can result in negative headlines and painful slots on consumer television programmes. So those complex departments of old where the reception or switchboard was seen to report to the head of communication perhaps knew a thing or two. They were a particular feature of the public sector. In order to be able to recruit and retain staff at a sufficiently senior level, unwieldy departments often grew up around the public relations and marketing function. It was not uncommon for typing pools and reprographic departments to be included in the communication function's remit.

The extremely complex activities of Vertex, which provides services for a wide range of mainly public sector bodies, reports to marketing. Here the internal audiences can even include staff on the authority's own payroll as well as those transferred across from former employing bodies.

IT and knowledge management

It goes without saying that technology has transformed internal communication in recent years. Getting to grips with HTML and its cousins is the bane of many a communicator's life and it can be tempting to hand this over to the IT department.

Another recent buzz phrase has been 'knowledge management'. A few rather imaginative technology experts have seen this as an extra for their armoury. For those who have missed this trend, it involves persuading staff to share their knowledge with their colleagues. This can result in an unmanageable mass of data which proves the point that data are not necessarily information, and information in its turn does not always convert to knowledge.

However, some IT managers also think that being able to crack the code means they should manage the information. It is one step from there to managing the information output. Database-generated websites are a real advance but they can overlook the basic principles of effective communication. A few multi-talented individuals may make the leap into design and in some cases to content, but this could explain why the worldwide web is littered with hard-to-use sites.

SO HUMAN RESOURCES OR PUBLIC RELATIONS?

Ultimately in the field of internal communication the two departments within which the function most often sits is either public relations or human resources. David Ashford (2001) devoted his Masters dissertation to the question of the function's most natural home.

His findings suggest that in larger companies internal communications mostly has a reporting line into public relations, whereas small organizations link it to human resources. He also found that human resources and public relations practitioners take different approaches to internal communication.

He suggests that historically human resources and corporate communications evolved from their origins as tactical support – personnel and public relations. Developing into today's more strategically focused function has led to a battle for the boardroom.

David Ashford identified five models for internal communications: alignment with human resources; alignment with public relations; division of responsibility between public relations and human resources; reporting directly to the chief executive; or full integration and shared responsibility between human resources and public relations.

There were different views as to the purpose of internal communications depending on which function the respondent came from. Human resources executives regarded employee communications 'to be information sharing and empowerment with the ultimate goal of improving job effectiveness'.

When it comes to change management, both sides were insistent that both departments should work together but within their specific roles.

Those who had come into internal communications from a journalistic background were adamant that human resources people should not be actually delivering the messages as they had a tendency to complicate issues. The danger here is that human resources could become the policy driver while public relations just delivered at the tactical end.

Where a public relations reporting line was established this was seen to be a good thing. Public relations has a remit across the whole business and can demonstrate an understanding of the need for consistency in internal and external messages.

Quite a few of the respondents felt that where the internal communicator or department reported to did not matter too much. One possible outcome is for public relations and human resources practitioners to be drawn closer together.

Wherever the internal communication function sits, it should be delivered in a sensitive manner which is attuned to the organization's needs. See Figure 5.1 for what can only be described as a 'dream' organizational chart.

Figure 5.1 *The internal communication function – the ideal structure: a theoretical ideal internal communication department with ideal reporting lines*

KEY POINTS TO REMEMBER

- Internal communication should be a key responsibility of the CEO.
- Internal communication was commonly found in corporate communication departments but also possibly human resources or marketing.
- Internal communication specialists need good cross-organizational links wherever based.
- Consistency with external messages is essential.
- Where it sits is not important, being sensitively attuned to the organization's needs is.

6

Outsourcing the internal communication function

THE BUSINESS CASE

Something of a barometer for the health of the wider business community is offered by keeping track of the number of in-house communications people who suddenly reappear on the horizon in the guise of roving consultant. When times are rather better there tends to be an influx of people into in-house positions. This appears true for both internal and external communication.

As is the case with public relations generally, organizations both large and small may decide to use external expertise for a variety of reasons. This chapter will look at the pros and cons, including economic arguments and also how existing in-house staff may react under certain circumstances and the reasons why.

Even organizations with quite large internal communications functions feel the need to draw on external expertise from time to time. Some very large employers keep a permanent roster of freelance consultants who can be called on to work through what is now deemed to be everyday change management.

Others may well call on a pool of communication consultancies to pitch for individual pieces of work or even whole programmes. By and large they too are working on the implementation end of things, producing the publications, the events, the website and the video.

But occasionally it is possible to find an example where it is the strategic thinking which has been contracted out. This approach worries those who argue that going down that route can result in everything being treated as a series of one-off activities rather than a unified whole, for there is a view that the overall panoramic vision can only come from being situated in-house with the ear of the top management at least somewhere close by.

According to consultant Richard Gaunt, whoever does internal communications has to be in the loop at the highest level. They would be best positioned alongside the change agent in the company, be it the chief executive, human resources or whatever.

In his experience internal people often get hijacked to other activities, or are not devoted full time to it. Statistics for local government communicators suggest the majority spend no more than 30 per cent of their time on internal communication. As a result, the function will frequently lack focus and fall prey to the ills of procrastination and delay which can affect all organizations, only coming to the boil (if at all) when there is an emergency.

Richard Gaunt says that many internal communication people are inexperienced and untrained, having had a career elsewhere in the company (engineering, safety, secretarial) while others are graduates in media studies or public relations trying to apply advanced theoretical models to a bemused and sceptical company. He fears the programme will then get ditched at the first sight of a budget cut.

An external consultant on the other hand will make the time (within your budget constraints) to give concentrated attention to your internal communication issues, and it is in his or her interests to deliver on time.

A glance at the recruitment pages indicates that even junior help will not come cheap if it is to be situated in-house. Companies have to consider the cost of the recruitment and selection process. Depending on the seniority of the position this could prove expensive, especially if head hunters are commissioned. In addition to this there are salary costs and other expenses including pensions, National Insurance and other benefits. Even though there is a desire for newcomers to hit the ground running, the reality is few will. Some form of induction and ongoing training will also be required.

There are not-so-obvious costs too. Desks if not offices have to be found and equipment supplied. Bringing staff up to speed on any newly introduced technology is also a hidden extra. The knock-on effect goes on and on. Obviously this applies to any job but it is easy to see why an organization would think very carefully before going down the in-house route in the first place.

When using external consultancies the fee charged will cover a proportion of the overheads which are no longer the responsibility of the client. Spread over a number of clients, it is possible that the consultant may not cost quite so much over the long term as an in-house appointee.

This calculation may come unstuck depending on the nature of the consultancy being offered. More and more general public relations consultancies are tempted by, and are attempting to gain a foothold in, what they see as lucrative new territory. As there is a crossover from communication into organizational development, management consultants will also be operating in this field.

Chapter 21 is devoted to the nuts and bolts of purchasing external services, but to give you some idea according to the Chartered Institute of Public Relations consultant rates could be around £500 per day. This sounds reasonable for public relations advice but is still likely to be a huge leap in investment terms for organizations with not much money to spend.

Obviously it is a case of horses for courses. It is unlikely an organization needing a simple newsletter knocked out would want to pay that kind of money, but for a major change management project that needs to be up and running quickly it may be worth it.

What you are really paying for when consulting with the likes of Richard Gaunt is perhaps decades of expertise which is unlikely to be similarly matched straight off a degree course. So there can be an argument for occasionally stretching the budget to such extremes.

Consultants can be called on not only to give high-level strategic advice, but also to provide support to in-house people who have rather less personal experience on which to call. This can be time limited or rather more open-ended, if the latter clear guidelines are needed to ensure costs are contained. In the case of specialist services such as printing and photography an understanding is needed as to who is footing the bill.

WHAT CONSULTANCIES CAN OFFER

Consultancies, and for that matter sole practitioners, with sufficient experience and good contacts can effectively run the entire internal communications function on-site or at one remove. The more usual scenario is to contract out specific activities rather than the whole enterprise.

A diverse range of services can be for sale, ranging from satisfaction surveys through to board games. Technological solutions for the provision of websites, design of surveys or logistical management of employee conferences can save thousands of pounds and do away with some very boring tasks en route.

Many organizations have the design and production work for publications and videos carried out by external specialists. Those working for CIPR accredited consultancies often come with good-quality experience gained in working in other categories of media such as national and regional newspapers and magazines, or client side, that is within organizations in the public or commercial sector.

Change management involving staff relocating from across Europe to a base in the south-east of England was contracted out by DHL. The company which won the pitch carried out the organizational development work and the communications aspects to support the programme. Running the project across a number of other countries was a major part of the remit, and taking account of the different cultural norms was one of the biggest challenges.

Face-to-face interaction with employees can be a matter of concern not only for front-line supervisors but also for directors and other senior management. Some communications consultancies offer communications coaching.

So the range of activities which a company can buy in is incredibly varied, ranging from straightforward delivery to strategic advice and even delivery of both. Consultancy can be bought from quite large firms in terms of numbers through to sole traders operating alone or in partnership with others to deliver the entire package or their part of it. The choice depending on budget is yours.

REASONS TO BE CAUTIOUS

Your in-house person or team is preparing to work alongside the rather expensive consultancy team you have brought in to inject some fresh ideas. What could possibly go wrong?

There appears to be a downside to every upside! Even very experienced internal people could well get jittery when expensive suits hove into view. Appointing consultants can send a subliminal warning to incumbent staff that their jobs may be at risk or that their skills are in doubt.

Even where the consultant is working in an organization without in-house expertise there is still room for trouble. It is hard enough for a new postholder to convince organizational old hands that there is a good business case; it is even harder for external practitioners. Without careful planning your expensive consultants may be held back in their activities, which may prove unexpectedly expensive for you if the delays can be blamed on the internal end.

Confidentiality may also be an issue where consultants work with similar customers. Conversely, credentials may be viewed with doubt if there is no apparent previous experience in the field on which to draw. There could be fears that external agents might opt for the 'cookie cutter' approach. This is where consultancies have a particular approach which they will tailor the client to fit rather than vice versa.

GETTING THE BEST FROM YOUR CONSULTANCY

From time to time most in-house departments will want to call on expertise outside their own experience to bring in fresh and wider insights, or simply more muscle to get the job done. The pros and cons have been well rehearsed earlier in this chapter, as have the potential pitfalls to avoid. But there are ways of working with external specialists which should ensure a satisfactory experience for all. These are covered more fully in Chapter 21, but some brief pointers follow below.

The starting point should be to go back to the organization's objectives and current strategy and establish what it is that should be done to meet them. Be clear as to what it is you actually want and be sensible about who you invite to tender. Keeping numbers of quotes to a realistic level will help boost your credibility with external contractors and make taking the right decision much simpler.

Before looking outside, take an inventory of the skills base offered internally as this is often a cheaper option. Determine who internally will oversee the delivery of activity and who will be responsible on a day-to-day basis.

Prepare a decent brief and check that it means something outside your department and organization – your internal jargon may be incomprehensible to everyone else.

Be clear about what you are agreeing to in terms of time and budget. Draw up and sign contracts and keep to them. Build in some flexibility at the beginning to allow for consultants learning your organization. Keep consultants well briefed on any changes that become necessary.

It is also important to build in to any contract a carefully worded clause on how you expect your chosen consultancy to handle issues around confidentiality. You need to strike a balance between benefiting from their expertise in your specialist field without the worry that your trade secrets will be shared.

In conclusion, consultancies should complement rather than duplicate the skills of yourself and your internal team. You need also to ensure that the consultancy's own culture complements that of your organization. Be realistic about costs and keep a close eye on budgets. Be clear as to the complexity of the issue(s) you wish the consultancy to address. Clarify their core skills and whether they are those of the individuals who will work on the account or simply the fancy suits from the boardroom sent to impress at the pitch. And most importantly ask yourself – do you like them, can you work with them?

KEY POINTS TO REMEMBER

- Consultants can supplement internal skills.
- Consultants are useful for implementing programmes.
- Highly experienced consultants can be used to provide strategic advice but usually this should be an internally sited expertise.
- External consultants need to be kept informed.
- It is possible to contract out the whole function, but consider the rationale carefully.
- Be clear with the brief.
- Cover all eventualities in the contract (confidentiality, termination, deadlines, etc).
- Provide and maintain effective reporting channels.

7

How the legal framework fits in

Internal communicators are as affected by the legal framework of the country as their external communication counterparts. When working across different borders it also pays to be aware of local regulation and legislation that may make a difference.

This section will look at the general legal framework that may have an impact on the work done within the internal communications function. It will look at aspects of workplace rules and laws which may not at first sight seem particularly pertinent, before turning to the European picture and what lies ahead. The rationale for including what will appear to be a substantial amount of human relations law, including that on discrimination, is the need to be aware of it when drafting materials or advising on programmes. A good place to start in the search for advice, for Chartered Institute of Public Relations members at least, is the members-only section of the institute's website (www.cipr.co.uk). Useful books include Howard's *The Practice of Public Relations* (1988) and the latest edition of *Essential Law for Journalists* by Welsh and Greenwood (2003). The authors are indebted to specialist media and communications law firm Olswang for assistance with information included in this chapter. Further information is also available on the Olswang website, www.olswang.com.

GENERAL COMMUNICATION MINEFIELDS

Defamation: libel and slander

You may imagine it would be less likely for an internal communicator to fall foul of defamation laws, but in today's more litigious environment it could well happen. There are several ways in which the law of libel may impact on internal communications work.

For example, publication of the wrong photograph to illustrate a point could result in a claim being made by individuals either internally or externally based. One personal close shave for the author happened in the late 1980s in a London hospital. Purely illustrative photographs were taken of an isolation ward for an internal publication. A misplaced caption meant that a clearly identifiable individual could have argued it had been implied he had a particular condition, which he did not. The condition had potentially unfortunate sexual connotations. In terms of libel, there is no distinction between a publication intended only for distribution within an organization and one which is circulated to the wider public. Liability arises in any circumstance where a defamatory statement is published to a third party (not the subject) – even if it is only one colleague. Fortunately for this author, the narrow circulation of the publication to only the public relations department meant the risk of discovery of the libel was reduced, and this averted an expensive trip to the courts. Thorough proofreading would have prevented this libel.

More commonly the problem will arise with written or spoken statements rather than images. Be particularly careful of claims made about third parties or organizations – check these out with the party concerned. If you believe there is a potentially libellous statement about a third party it is of paramount importance you give them an opportunity to comment (although this alone is not a defence to an action). If in doubt leave it out.

Defamation is the publication of a statement which lowers a person in the estimation of 'right-thinking members of society' (ie the typical reader or recipient of the statement). Libel covers statements in written or permanent form; slander, spoken or transitory. Websites, intranets and e-mails are included. In the case of electronic media, take care where staff are able to add their own material to sites – any difficulties arising from untrue statements will become the responsibility of the organization. Office banter circulating by internal e-mail is a major risk. In 1997 Norwich Union paid Western Provident Association £450,000 damages plus costs after staff circulated rumours about the rival company via the internal e-mail. The company was liable for activities (even though unauthorized) of its employees. A strict policy on the use of e-mail is therefore essential.

The law presumes the statement which is disputed is false, unless the defendant can prove it is true. This can be extremely difficult, or even impossible with the evidence available. Remember the defendant also has to prove the truth of what the average reader thought the article meant – not what the defendant might have intended to say – so take care of ambiguity or unintended meanings. In your defence you might claim that the statement is true or fair comment (based on true facts), or that the information is privileged which usually applies to Parliament and court proceedings. Make good use of any legal advice to which your organization has access.

Copyright, registered designs and patents

We have already referred to the possibility of libel in imagery. Much more likely is a claim for misuse of copyright owned by a photographer. Unless your organization actually employs the photographer as an employee or has obtained a detailed signed contract transferring the rights, copyright of images rest with the photographer.

Be very careful about downloading images off a website unless it is clear they can be used. It is far better to go to a photographic library, many of which are online. It also pays to inform the photographer or the library of the uses to which the images will be put as part of the briefing process. You should also consult about any change of use at that or some later date. If the photographer owns the copyright they may object to certain uses.

Using an image more than once may also incur an extra fee, so any contract should formally take account of this. This also applies to the use of photo library shots – you will get billed for extra uses.

As a matter of courtesy if nothing else it is a good idea to credit the artist and/or source of an image even if you have paid for this. Good manners may reduce bills – legal ones that is.

The law does not protect ideas as such, it can only protect the expression of those ideas in written, artistic or other form. Copyright exists automatically and applies only if the work is original and then for a certain period of time (eg literary copyright in words, such as in this book, lasts from the moment of creation until 70 years after the author's death). Copyright is breached where a 'substantial part' of the work is used or reproduced without permission of the copyright owner. The Copyright, Design and Patents Act 1988 has been amended to take account of European Union-inspired harmonization. Keep in mind that copyright laws may still be different from country to country and this could have a bearing not just on publication of information from another country, but also anything being published across a number of countries.

An aggrieved party might seek an injunction forbidding further infringement, ask for damages and an order for offending copies to be surrendered. Defences might be that there is no copyright in the work or that the person complaining is not the rightful owner of the copyright.

Another way of protecting intellectual property is by applying for a trademark. These can be granted over words and phrases, pictures and designs, colours and even smells. The trademark allows its owner to exploit it exclusively in particular areas of use. The English language seems peppered with trade names that have become generic terms (Hoover for vacuum cleaner). To save at the very least hours of a law lecture from a passing pedant it is worth finding substitutes from everyday language. Trademark protection incidentally is for a limited period.

Plagiarism is a related problem, certainly in any area which touches on the academic world. If in producing copy you refer to other people's documents, quote them thoroughly and accurately. It is permissible to reproduce a copyright work if it is either an insubstantial part, or if it is being used solely for private research. Commercial use will not be covered by this latter exception. It should be clear you are not laying claim to the ideas of another. If nothing else it is good manners to give credit where it is due.

Breach of confidence

Misuse of ideas or information received in confidence from someone else can be the subject of an action for breach of confidence. For example, one client may object to their information being used for the benefit of another. Conversely this could apply if a consultant felt a proposal or plan had been used without consent or payment. This latter can be difficult to argue on grounds of the offending item having to be an exact copy of their original work. It will assist if you require clients to whom you pitch ideas to enter into a confidentiality agreement, or at the very least make clear that the information you share is confidential and may not be reused. It is of course bad form to pass off someone else's ideas as your own.

Equally it is at the very least bad form to relay to other parties information given to you in confidence. This could have been the result of a badly drafted brief and would apply equally to those given to in-house practitioners as well as externally based consultants. Seek clarification of anything that causes concern, checking discreetly with others in appropriate positions where possible.

A different kind of breach of confidence can be where an aggrieved member of staff has gone outside the organization, possibly to the mass or specialist media, to complain of alleged malpractice. Whistleblowers (see also 'Health and Safety' section), where they can show they have acted in good faith and it is in the public interest to disclose the confidential information, are likely to have a good defence against an action for breach of confidence or unfair dismissal, and the resulting publicity will do no good for the organization's standing or for internal morale. An internal communicator who has built a sound reputation at all levels of an organization may be able to act as an internal barometer, picking up on concerns before they reach such a critical stage.

A special subset of breach of confidence has also developed to protect the individual's privacy. In effect, it is now unlawful to misuse private personal confidential information. This may be recorded information such as medical and health details, political or religious beliefs, or it could be photographs taken in private places.

For this reason it is good practice and in some sectors mandatory to secure informed consent for photography or filming of the public. Especial care needs to be exercised when handling situations involving children, but also adults who may, by reason of mental health issues, be unable to give informed consent. A consent form can be easily drawn up and should be phrased in simple but clear language because those signing must understand what they are agreeing to.

Competitions

To liven up publications and encourage reader involvement it can be tempting to come up with a competition. Be particularly careful when drafting rules, especially where some external audiences might be included. The Institute of Sales Promotion (see Appendix 4 for address) has more detail on this complex area.

Contract law

Law on contract may apply in a number of ways, particularly if you yourself are a consultant, or as an in-house person are using subcontractors to carry out work. A consultant can also subcontract work but retains the responsibility for that work. It is worth keeping records including invoices for up to six years after the contract is concluded, as action for breach of contract can be taken for that period.

As a consultant it is important to ensure all agreements entered into with and on behalf of a client are carefully worded. When booking rooms or ordering print work or photography, it is relatively common for suppliers to bill the consultant direct who then charges the client. However, if the client defaults on the payment the consultant will be liable, unless it has been made very clear that the agreement is directly between client and supplier and the consultant is acting only as an agent of the client. You may only enter into agreements as an agent for your client if you have the proper authority to do so.

Employers or clients will be liable for the acts of employees or agents carried out in the course of their employment. If the act is of a criminal nature, liability would only apply if the act was carried out under the employer's instructions.

Any contract for services implies a duty of care to the client. When giving a reference for an employee or supplier there is a duty of reasonable care, so these should be drafted with caution. Painting too rosy a picture can be as bad as the opposite. Remember the risks of defamation when giving references.

IN THE WORKPLACE ITSELF

Employment legislation/good practice

The way in which business procedures and relationships are conducted in the workplace could come under public scrutiny should an individual be disciplined and/or dismissed. It is worth keeping informed of any changes in this area and of the exceptions that might apply, as not all line managers will be sufficiently informed to have acted according to the law.

Employers may place restrictive clauses in the employment contract to attempt to prevent former employees being able on behalf of future employers to make use of information gained while in their earlier employment, or to 'poach' clients or staff. The ex-employee may argue it restricts their freedom of employment. Usually such a restrictive clause will be successful as long as it is not unreasonable in its scope or duration.

Employees can now bring a claim of unfair dismissal if they have been in the organization's employ for a year, but there are circumstances under which they can act sooner. These occasions usually relate to discriminatory practices or where early dismissal was instituted for no other reason than to circumvent legal requirements.

Incidents of gross misconduct may mean employers do not have to go through the lengthy proceedings usually required of them when seeking to dismiss. What could constitute gross misconduct is an area of some debate, and again could lead in the direction of the employment tribunal.

Health and safety

In heavy industry and construction trades, strict guidelines are usually in place for the protection of the worker and their colleagues. Some responsibility does fall to the individual to wear protective clothing as appropriate and to act sensibly in areas of risk. That does not, however, exonerate the employer from providing the necessary equipment for the safe performance of the work or from ensuring the environment is safe. Failure to do so can result in prolonged media coverage of a negative nature which will involve inquests (in the case of death), inquiry (death and injury) and court cases which could result in imprisonment, hefty fines and compensation.

Covering such incidents in company publications is likely to provide a particular challenge.

Where the internal communicator is more likely to be involved on a day-to-day basis is when issues of health and safety are dealt with in advance of problems developing. At BMW Plant Hams Hall a video was made on the subject of cleaning to emphasize its importance to everyone. Practical tips on safe lifting and handling and also safe use of such seemingly innocuous equipment as computers may also be a proactive way of averting problems.

Health and safety can also be extended into more general workplace welfare and can encompass harassment and bullying. Despite official help for those who blow the whistle on poor practice, tribunals and other court hearings are still a too-common outcome. There were 1,200 claims under the Public Interest Disclosure Act up until February 2003 according to Gaymer (2003).

Trying to move away from this, some organizations have put in confidential hotlines to encourage staff to see the internal route as the preferred one.

Anticipating forthcoming law can bring competitive advantage and enhanced reputation, as global mining giant Rio Tinto surely demonstrates. For the past couple of years the company has been running a programme which encourages employees to confidentially and, if required, anonymously report any issue of concern. Calls are taken by an independent third party and passed to two senior members of staff to investigate. A summary of the call report and any subsequent investigation and action then goes to the global chief executive. This is regarded as the ultimate expression of corporate transparency, a step in the right direction for good governance.

Trying to implement a programme like that across different cultures, governments and languages is quite challenging. The idea came from the CEO, and the company wants to make sure all activity is carried out in the safest manner, that all problems are identified at the earliest possible stage and appropriate actions taken.

Communications Advisor and the programme's global coordinator, Mike Moser, says: 'Safety is one of the most important issues for Rio Tinto and although we have rigorous safety standards to which we operate, should an employee have any concerns in this area, we would like them expressed. The programme is being positioned as a last resort communications channel when all existing ones – such as an open-door policy or face-to-face meetings – have been exhausted. In light of recent UK legislation all major organizations will need similar programmes.'

To show how seriously it takes safety, in what after all must rate as one of the potentially most dangerous industrial sectors, Rio Tinto requires even a twisted ankle to be included in accident reports. Figures for all these reports are made public on the company's safety website and summarized in its annual safety and environment report.

Not all bullying and harassment in the workplace stems from an attempt to cover up unsafe practice, but could be the unfortunate extension of a particular culture that the company may have fostered inadvertently. Pressured environments where difficult-to-reach targets are set could be a breeding ground for this kind of behaviour. The internal communicator needs to pay attention to the tone of materials they produce to ensure they are not adding to any problem.

Monitoring staff behaviour is a particularly tricky area. Privacy too is of growing concern and there remain issues around the personal use of telephones. A bank monitored calls for a day and found only 10 per cent related to work. The latest trend is now related to e-mail and internet use and abuse, and there have already been several high-profile cases regarding teams and individuals sacked for downloading pornography. (See also the earlier section on the risk of e-mail defamation.) Staff should be informed if calls and internet-based activity are to be monitored.

On a more positive note internal communicators may find themselves explaining benefits to staff as part of their work. Current issues around pension rights are spilling over into the external media environment and need to be addressed internally.

Work–life balance

Drawing the line between what part of an employee's life is in the public or employer's domain and what is not is becoming increasingly difficult. Basic issues such as working hours have in recent years been the focus of directives from Europe. Parents of both sexes now have greater rights for time off paid or unpaid during certain periods of their children's lives. Greater flexibility is apparently the desire of larger numbers of employees. These requirements may be rather time sensitive as during a recession there may be less emphasis on rights and more on hanging on to the job.

How you dress is also becoming an issue worthy of a tribunal as recent media coverage has demonstrated. Dress codes may seem eminently sensible when faced with a young staff determined to dress in torn denim on an exhibition stand, but proceed with caution, especially if the rules cannot be applied equally across both sexes and to individuals whose clothing is part of their religious beliefs.

Diversity

Since 2 December 2003 legislation outlawing discrimination on the grounds of religion and belief extended the rather limited racial discrimination legislation in this area. Your organization will need to provide appropriate facilities for different religious groups, such as prayer mats, if it affords a different religious group equivalent privileges, and with increasing diversity in the workplace this will become even more of an issue. Your publications will also need to be designed to take account of the need for balance between different groups.

The December 2003 deadline was shared with regulations which apply not just to gender but also to sexual orientation. Disability legislation which requires every reasonable effort to be made to make the workplace fully accessible was further extended in 2004, while age regulations will be added in December 2006.

This latter is of particular concern with the increasing focus on anticipated shortfalls in pensions and the perceived need for working lives to be lengthened to compensate. It will no longer be acceptable personnel practice to allow a less effective member of staff to mark time to retirement if that is no longer likely to occur at a fixed time. Workers currently past retirement age have been resorting to the courts for some time now to enable them to work beyond statutory retirement age. Future legislation is likely to introduce rules which will allow individuals to work beyond the traditional retirement age of 65, if they choose.

It is entirely possible to go too far in this direction and wind up being accused of being too politically correct. Chapter 11 covers managing the needs and attitudes of different staff groups (in terms of age, gender, ethnicity, culture, etc) rubbing up against each other in the workplace. Striking a balance between good manners, what is realistic in terms of the size of the organization, and the letter and spirit of the law should be sufficient. Maintenance of good relationships with your human resources and legal colleagues is therefore essential.

Data protection

Data protection legislation has been extended beyond computerized records to include paper-based files. This means that all personal data about a living individual which is held or processed is subject to complex rules about when and how it may be used.

Public sector organizations have long known how to handle sensitive and confidential information, and commercial enterprises could well learn from them. (Public authorities are, in addition, now also subject to the provision of the Freedom of Information Act 2000 which allows individuals to require disclosure of information the public authority holds.) Human resources colleagues should also be well versed in the precise implications of data protection law.

An individual attending an interview can now request all notes taken at the proceedings to be handed over. Scurrilous comment on dress sense (or what could be construed as such) is unlikely to read well at a tribunal.

Scrupulous notes on all proceedings relating to an individual should be kept but should be drafted in a careful way with potential litigation in mind. Be prepared for whatever is written to be requested at some stage.

All organizations which process personal data (which is likely to be almost any firm with employee records at least) are required to be registered with the Information Commissioner. The application form for data protection registration is a good place to start in attempting to establish a framework for policy in this area. The legislation also applies to a whole range of other information which may have been stored concerning individuals or organizations. It is good practice to review all files and establish whether material needs to be kept.

Human rights

Since the coming into force of the Human Rights Act 1998, the courts have been obliged to interpret all legislation and case law in such a way as to ensure that the rights and obligations of the European Convention on Human Rights are observed. This now colours the entirety of the law. The most important rights in the context of communication are Article 8 – the right to respect for private and family life, home and correspondence; and Article 10 – the right to freedom of expression.

Stock Exchange

Because of the impact of price-sensitive information on share price, the Stock Exchange requires to hear of major changes in the workplace from you first, before you can tell the rest of the world.

It all has to be done with military precision: the Stock Exchange at 7.30 am, then an immediate flurry of e-mails and text messaging to precipitate cascade briefings to staff literally minutes later, often as they arrive for work. Informing staff of a major change in the business or worse, that they have been made redundant, by text or e-mail is extremely poor practice.

Consultation Directive/works councils

All this is brought sharply into focus by what is likely to prove the biggest shake-up in the world of internal communication for quite some time. The European Commission's Information and Consultation Directive was implemented in the UK in March 2005.

As stated in the Chartered Institute of Public Relations policy document on the subject, it establishes a right to new minimum standards for workforce communication and involvement in large firms. It makes a basic case for the fair treatment of people at work.

The directive applies to undertakings or establishments (either business, or public and private organizations carrying out economic activity not necessarily for gain) in the European community. It is being phased in so that it applies to undertakings with 150 or more employees from March 2005, those with 100 or more employees by March 2007, and those with 50 or more by March 2008.

The directive gives employees the right to be informed about the business's economic situation, and informed and consulted about work prospects, and major changes in work organization or contracts, including redundancies and transfers from one organization to another.

Information giving and consultation has to take place at an appropriate time and at the right level of management. Usually it will be done via employee representatives. Having received the information they may meet the employer, present their opinion and expect a reasoned response.

Employers and employees may agree differing procedures. It is for the individual member states to determine the way they go about this. Employers can withhold information where its disclosure may harm the company or they may require it to be kept secret by the employee representatives.

Previously employees were only entitled to consultation limited to collective redundancies, transfers of undertakings, health and safety, and in large multinational companies through European works councils.

This framework is already in operation in other European countries and, despite similarly strict money market structures, has been made to work. A recent survey of 24 multinational companies' experiences of works councils has been very positive, according to legal firm Hammonds.

Speaking at the CIPR's then Internal Communications Group in 2002 (now Internal Communication Alliance) lawyer Makbool Javaid asserted that the directive also reflects the very clear differences between British and European corporate culture. The UK approach has been to prefer to communicate directly to staff and to control the agenda. The European line opts for the representation model which concentrates on negotiation and discussion with employees on decision making.

Such a fundamental change in approach is likely to open up more opportunities for communicators who have the trust of both senior management and the workforce. Being aware of the legislative framework as a whole is the first step towards building this necessary confidence.

Key points to remember regarding the Information and Consultation Directive were set out by Paul Massie from National Grid Transco at a meeting of the Internal Communication Alliance held in spring 2004. He said the directive will not be:

- set in stone;
- specific about the arrangement your organization should actually make.

It would however be:

- a recognition of the right to information and consultation;
- a general framework setting out minimum standards.

It would require employers to:

- inform about recent and probable developments in company activities and the economic situation;
- inform and consult about decisions likely to lead to substantial changes in contracts or in the way work is organized;
- inform and consult about employment prospects.

Paul Massie said the UK had a strong business case for adopting the directive. It could be argued to be essential for 'creating high performance workplaces' and building 'a culture of trust, co-operation, mutual respect and innovation'. It also would improve employee satisfaction and improve management decision making.

In practice the directive means organizations will have to inform and consult their workforce on a far greater range of topics. Employee rights to information and consultation have also been greatly extended. Such informing and consultation needs to be conducted through employee representatives and there has to be representation of the whole workforce not simply those covered by trade union membership.

Research on behalf of the Internal Communication Alliance in early 2004 found that at that point 85 per cent knew little or nothing about the regulations and even more were scarcely prepared for them.

Organizations which fail to agree a valid structure could face a fine of £75,000. So how should organizations be preparing themselves? Paul Massie says they should audit their current industrial relations environment and check what workforce agreements already exist, and review them and the management decision-making process.

He believes the directive offers internal communicators the chance to 'drive employee involvement, participation and dialogue'. It provides an opportunity to review and improve existing two-way channels of communication and opens up the possibility of closer partnership with human resources.

Freedom of Information Act 2000

Since 1 January 2005, some 100,000 public authorities across the UK have been required to change the way in which they respond to and provide information to the general public. This legislation is intended to help the public understand how such authorities carry out their duties, make decisions and spend the money they receive. The list of public authorities affected by the legislation is wide, and it can require the authority to disclose not only information about their own organization but also information they hold about third parties. The Act may therefore have implications for commercial companies too, particularly those who are regulated by a public body or who participate in public–private partnerships.

Exemption clauses will cover information including that which may be deemed likely to affect national security, involve personal data or commercial confidentiality. However, it is feasible that the legislation could be used indirectly to flush out some information which could affect companies.

Organizations which have devised appropriate record-keeping procedures which are sufficiently flexible to take account of requests for information should be able to cope with this latest piece of legislation.

KEY POINTS TO REMEMBER

- Be careful of accidental libel or slander; ignorance is no excuse.
- Consent forms for photography, film and audio formats are essential.
- Check copy as widely as possible.
- Be careful of third-party generated material on websites – responsibility rests with the organization.
- Clarify ownership of copyright to images through use of contracts.
- Keep files in good order in case of future disputes on contracts.
- Be clear through use of contracts who is responsible for suppliers' bills.
- Keep up to date on employment and health and safety legislation.
- Diversity is an ever-expanding field: watch for age to join religion, gender, sexual orientation and race.
- Major workplace changes must be communicated to the Stock Exchange first.
- The European Information and Consultation Directive will affect even quite small companies by 2008.
- Use the directive as a positive opportunity to build trust between management and workforce with major benefits for the bottom line.
- The Freedom of Information Act has greatest impact on public authorities, but those private companies providing any information to public authorities need to watch out.

8

The channels, vehicles and activities

Now the fun bit. This chapter effectively acts as a menu of options as regards communication vehicles. There can be a tendency to focus too much on the media and lend a bit too much credence to the Marshall McLuhan much-misquoted slogan, 'the medium is the message'. It may also be why some management continues to see communicators as mere messengers or purveyors. Putting that argument to one side it is worth being aware of the many ways you can communicate with your workforce if you only had the budget!

This chapter will touch on each main group of activities with the emphasis on when to use them. The 'how' will be covered in more detail in Chapters 13–21.

WHAT IS THE MESSAGE?

Before looking at today's options for media selection, here are some simple guidelines to assist management in crafting those all important messages.

The selection of media should not be the highest ranked priority on the list when planning a strategy for internal communication.

Senior management should first be encouraged to think about what it is that needs to be communicated. A very few key messages should be distilled because there can be a temptation to swamp the internal public with far too many ideas all at once. A desire to cover all the bases simultaneously can lead to as much confusion as offering no information at all.

Simplicity should also be the guiding principle behind the delivery of the specific messages. Information should be kept simple and presented in language with which the selected audience is comfortable. Boardroom jargon may not translate too well down at the call centre, but will be appropriate at senior and middle management levels.

As with external communication programmes, internal audiences should be segmented to assist in the effective and timely delivery of appropriate information. Timing would obviously be a factor when delivering information that could have an impact on Stock Exchange ratings. In this example senior managers would be briefed before those in customer-facing or more front-line positions.

Just because your organization has always produced a glossy magazine does not mean that this is the only way information can be communicated. Media appropriate to the message, its timing and the needs and preferences of the audience should be considered.

It is unwise for any large organization to put all its eggs in one media basket and just use one medium. Even the smallest of organizations is likely to be using more than one approach to communicate with its internal audiences. What follows should be seen as an opportunity to take a more holistic approach to communication and adopt multiple rather than solo media.

A good communications strategy recognizes the strengths and weaknesses of each medium and uses it appropriately to ensure lateral as well as top-down and bottom-up communication. A house journal or video should be seen as a tactic in the strategy rather than the strategy itself.

FACE TO FACE – ONE TO ONE

Often overlooked, but according to all the surveys still the most valued form of communication by employees across all sectors, is face-to-face, one-to-one communication.

However, there can be a negative side. Senior management can often make assumptions that a corporate stance is understood by all in the same way; this can be a dangerous position to adopt. It is necessary to check there really is mutual understanding on critical issues.

If management has chosen not to practise one-to-one communication or is not doing so comprehensively enough, the staff concerned will find their own channels for plugging the gaps in their knowledge. What they hear on the grapevine or round the water cooler may not be the real position but it will in their view have to suffice.

A wily communicator will set up a more officially approved version of the grapevine by developing 'champions' to ensure the right information is getting out, but this needs to be handled very carefully to overcome any suspicions or hostility.

A technique from the human resources or organizational development end of the spectrum is mentoring, buddying or coaching. There are shades of opinion as to whether mentoring and coaching actually constitute different things. The relationship can be very structured or quite informal and these days does not in fact require much in terms of face-to-face meetings, as e-mail can suffice to maintain contact.

There are tools designed to help managers interact more effectively with those they come into contact with on a daily basis. The emphasis is on positive rather than negative feedback, and the opportunity to apply the criteria of success to other areas of practice.

Behavioural change which can improve one-to-one exchanges was achieved with no hurt feelings by international development charity Plan which invited actors in to conduct role-play. An extreme version of an ordinary exchange between a European fundraising person and a colleague based in an overseas project was played out. By making people laugh, some serious points were made about not making assumptions and how to negotiate successfully beyond them.

Although face to face in a one-to-one situation is the stated preferred mode by staff, it will not always fit the bill. It is most effective when messages are relatively simple and the opportunity it provides for the listener to give feedback instantly provides an excellent way of checking understanding and absorption. Messages should therefore be simple and repeated as necessary.

One to ones are most likely to be used when briefing individual team members and to check on progress on work in progress.

FACE TO FACE – EN MASSE

There are obviously occasions when a message has to be delivered to more than one member of staff, and internal communicators are more likely to become involved in preparing the materials for such mass opportunities. Simplicity remains crucial whatever the size of the group but the larger it becomes the more supporting material such as audio-visual tools and information packs will be required. Materials may need to be tweaked to meet the needs of different levels of an organization or different abilities. Content is most likely focused on business news and developments. It should, in an ideal world, be the way bad news about company performance is delivered. However, individual bad news such as redundancy should not be delivered impersonally but in one-to-one, face-to-face situations (texts to mobile phones and e-mails do not fit the bill).

Some companies put a huge amount of effort into running effective roadshows for groups of staff selected on a geographical or a business area basis. This structured approach ensures everyone gets the required and consistent message at some point. Video can be added to the mix as a spur for discussion. Using a mix of approaches ensures the message is emphasized.

Where it is just business as usual it is important that there is a point to the meeting and a clear agenda. Some organizations hold regular cascade briefing sessions which require key messages to be established by the board and then filtered down through the management levels and back up again. Feedback is not simply one-way as the executive team gives its response to employee comments through the team briefing.

There is scope too for a more personalized approach. Employees from across the North Tees and Hartlepool NHS Trust are also invited on a randomly selected basis to lunch sessions with directors. These are no holds barred, and if questions are not answered on the spot the query is followed up after the lunch. The response is fed back to the attendees in a memo despatched through the internal mail system.

Walking the business is an important way of keeping top managers in touch with the ground floor. At the Churchill Insurance group managers have to work at the 'coalface' several times a year, thereby debunking the 'special occasion' notion. In BP senior managers spend a day working at a petrol station. This helps them understand what is happening at the front line of the business.

Consider holding meetings at the local equivalent of a Starbucks café. Such a place would provide neutral territory for the meeting and provides space and 'quiet' for thinking away from telephones.

But it is not necessary to leave the office to achieve a relaxed environment as charity Plan discovered when it introduced 'brown-bag lunches' where you bring your lunchtime sandwiches to an informal meeting. The charity's Norma Johnston reports that the meetings are a mix of organizational housekeeping and important announcements, and a chance to hear how colleagues in the field actually deliver developmental programmes. Debate is encouraged by the communications staff and the sessions have been welcomed by staff who rarely visit programme countries to see Plan's work for themselves.

Again these sessions act almost in the manner of a physical manifestation of a publication. The 'show and tell' aspect aids understanding but also sugars the pill of other more mundane but critical matters for discussion.

Mass face-to-face meetings can be used effectively to disseminate crucial messages which need to be delivered in the same way and at the same time to a large group. Building a slot for regular meetings can overcome perceived communication vacuums but it is important than the information relayed is worthwhile, otherwise such activities can become discredited among key audiences.

PRINT

From newsletters to magazines via pay packet communication the value of an easily portable communication vehicle and its function as an organ of record should not be dismissed. Tips on content, design and dissemination appear in Chapter 15 while Chapter 16 concentrates on purchasing the necessary elements.

The demise of the printed word has long been predicted but is showing no immediate signs of happening. Companies which abandoned print in favour of intranet and e-mail bulletins have added it back into the mix. Like many other organizations the BBC maintains both, using the print publication for reflection and the intranet for immediate news items.

Publications should be content driven and could profitably take their inspiration from the news-stands. Rather too many publications produced for internal audiences do not have the production values and, therefore, the appeal of publications employees can buy off site.

LE (formerly London Electricity) Group's publication is a very high-quality full-colour publication with articles generated from all ends of the organization. Junior employees are encouraged to submit interviews conducted with senior management, thereby demonstrating a commitment to listening to and involving employees in a very active manner. A look through recent issues shows some distinctly non-journalistic types making a credible go at grilling top managers.

Publications are an excellent way of ensuring important messages are stressed and elaborated. They can serve as support for face-to-face activities, expanding and explaining particular points. Equally publications can be used as launch pads for initiatives. Dispersed workforces not always able to attend or be reached by face-to-face activities can read about them at their leisure. Publications give time for reflection and feedback, and although obviously not as speedy as face-to-face communication, can be built in.

There is a wide range of publication formats to choose from. A full-blown newspaper, most likely to be tabloid rather than broadsheet these days, lends a newsy aspect to any publication and is particularly suitable for audiences which favour newspapers for their external news. As in their external counterparts, content can be a fine balance between topical news items and more reflective pieces.

Magazines may be deemed more suitable for the kind of workforce distilled from the readership of periodical-style publications. Production values are likely to be more sophisticated than newspapers and so will take longer to prepare. Up-to-the-minute material is less likely to feature in these and the emphasis will be on in-depth articles.

Newsletters can be put together rather more quickly than either newspapers and magazines and can be used to transmit more urgent messages. It is possible to have a balance of news and features in these but the balance is most likely to favour the former.

Less frequent and more difficult to describe in terms of format are employee versions of annual reports. Depending on the preference for newspaper, magazine or newsletter formats the organization may opt for any of these. Whatever is selected is likely to be somewhat smaller scale than the version produced for the markets. Alongside the accounts the annual report provides an opportunity for deeper reflection on the work of individual units. An injection of imagination in terms of design is critical for ensuring they are read rather than simply used as decorative bookends.

Publications therefore can be used as support materials for face-to-face communications activities. They are also useful for getting information out to hard-to-reach groups. Regular publications can be used to reiterate messages that have been disseminated in other formats.

BROADCAST AND AUDIO-VISUAL

As all good media studies graduates know, the moving image is more involving than static print. Broadcast can be quite expensive, although technological advances are likely to despatch video to the archives in favour of DVDs. This quite recent addition to the communicator's armoury of communication vehicles has the extra advantage of interactivity and is most likely to be used to supplement face-to-face activity rather than stand alone, although it can be a substitute particularly for dispersed workforces.

Content can include much of what would make a face-to-face meeting engaging. There can be a chance to see managers, hear their views, see products and perhaps (if they are featured) colleagues in other parts of the organization. If produced professionally these can prove quite costly but it is possible to turn cameraman with today's digital cameras.

Norwich Union Insurance produces a regular DVD programme every 12 weeks. Head of Internal Communications Denice Currie says it is a mix of business news and information, usually focused on a topical theme. The programmes are structured to continually reinforce the organization's three goals of 'service, morale, profit'. As these are potentially such costly items to produce it is critical for senior management to build in feedback mechanisms to ensure front-line managers are actually showing them at meetings.

There are very practical reasons for going down the DVD route. With 16,000 staff in 70 different locations Norwich Union Insurance felt DVD programmes were an effective way to create a sense of 'one-ness' via team viewings. The format also allows the viewer or presenter to select what they want to see, offering a real sense of personal choice and interactivity.

It would have been possible to move straight from standard VHS video to streaming to the individual's desktop via PC. However this, it was felt, would have cut out the possibility for team engagement with managers. Live broadcast to desktop can prove exciting but gives little time for reflection on messages and would need to be backed up with adequate support material.

Interactivity is offered by the giant plasma screens installed at BMWs Hams Hall plant. Staff can find out about company news during their breaks if they cannot get to a computer screen as part of their jobs.

Phone-ins, sometimes called radio broadcast, are still popular. The LE Group includes live phone-ins as part of a complex mix. Executive team members are put in the hot seat to take questions from all callers. Some questions are very technical, others are more prosaic. The responses appear to be honest and open, and even a touch of humour creeps in. One caller complained they had not received their free gift; the manager offered his as a substitute.

Video conferencing is rarely mentioned by communicators in the field. Sophie Austin of IBM feels the technology is not developed quite sufficiently to make it an entirely credible alternative for face-to-face meetings. It is often hard to read the expressions of individuals and the occasional time lapse can even make it hard to establish who is actually speaking at a given time. However, it is useful for keeping established networks in touch with each other.

Video can have a function in the training mix or as part of an overall communication mix, but is fast being superseded by DVD in the communications mix. Audio cassettes continue to be used quite extensively with dispersed workforces making use of drive and other down time. Messages should be simple and engaging – but not too engaging as many will be listening while driving.

INTERNET DRIVEN

It is hard to remember that intranets were very much the new gadgetry kid on the block even in the mid-1990s and as recently as 1999 only 65 per cent of companies used intranets. Chapter 19 gives more detail on the practicalities of internet-driven communication.

It is important to remember that screen-based media such as e-mail and intranet are not as easy to read as print publications. This is a particularly important point for communicators with diverse audiences. Older people and those with sight problems will have a particular problem. Perhaps technologists will crack that one in time.

LE Group reaches 4,000 employees through a mix of newspapers, meetings, newsletters, videos, posting information, intranet, audio conferences, mail information and video conferences. Its publications are branded Live Wire and this branding is carried through the print publication, online daily news and an e-magazine which incorporates video clips. The intranet contains just about everything to engage the visitor including jpegs, mpegs and flash-enabled animation.

Cable and Wireless's intranet is so impressive that its in-house editor is now talking about it to external customers. The company's experience gives some indication of what appears to be a trend away from enabling staff to establish their own content towards central coordination. Launched in 2001 it replaces what were six official and no fewer than 100 non-official sites.

Whilst the vast majority of employees have access to the intranet, the team of five in China receive a copy burnt to compact disc twice a year. There are no print versions of any communications materials within the organization – everything from newsletters to newsfeeds are accessed online.

Since the beginning of 2002 the C & W intranet has become much more business driven to ensure staff are focused on the needs of the business. The intranet home page includes the latest business-related news updated on a daily basis.

From a communications perspective, the intranet provides news and housekeeping material together with newsletters from top management. Everything the individual needs to do their job is located on the intranet, and different business areas have their own discussion groups.

But before you get carried away, content needs to be pared to the bone because reading on screen is likely to remain a problem for some time to come. Chapter 19 underscores the techniques that can make or break a site or internet-driven activity, although much depends on the preferences of your audience. E-mail newsletters, for instance, are a quick way to keep people in touch but should be used sparingly to avoid information overload.

Recently arrived in terms of new media is texting, which is naturally quite popular with younger members of staff. Sophie Austin, Internal Communications Consultancy Manager at IBM, uses it to alert far-flung employees to activities on other media. It seems to work: sales staff alerted to a phone-in programme made the effort to respond and the hit rate has surged. Texting was used throughout the campaign to remind staff to make the call. A similar technique can be used to alert managers to start cascade briefings around Stock Exchange-influenced communication and at times of mass redundancy.

Mobile phones can effectively keep every part of the workforce in touch with the centre on a constant basis. The third generation or 3G allows rather larger amounts of information to be shifted much more quickly than ever before. Images of a far better quality are also possible although the fourth generation expected later this decade will take this even further. Again it is important not to get carried away with the technology – not everyone will have it or feel comfortable using it for some time to come.

CORPORATE GLUE – GAMES, ETC

Getting people to make the connection between company messages and their own actions is something of a major challenge. Sometimes a straight-forward presentation fails to hit the mark, hence the need to resort to something unusual.

Credo designed a board game for Bass Brewers to get all their employees focused on their contribution to the bottom line. Based on a racetrack game complete with dice and miniature cars, the aim was to help staff make the connection between their actions and the effect on the team's overall performance. Apparently it met with as much enthusiasm in the board room as it did on the brewery floor where its underlying messages were equally well understood.

Managing Director Colin Sneath said that avoiding 'corporate speak' was probably what made it such a success as everyone understood the allegory. Boxes of the game can still be found years on!

Gimmicks can also be used to draw attention to seemingly boring but essential messages. Speaking at the Chartered Institute of Public Relations national conference in November 2003 Hamish Hayes of BSKyB demon-strated just how effective this could be, especially when dealing with a young audience. A top director in Scotland literally got on his bike and visited the team, dispensing ice cream as he went. Bags of chocolate coins were distributed to employees to encourage them to find out more about pensions – the uptake went from nil to a respectable level very quickly. These may seem highly irreverent if not downright irrelevant – but the quirkiness of the ideas hit the spot.

Organizations both large and small often take employees away from their everyday environment to try to improve networking and give them the mental space to think perhaps more creatively.

Among the many kinds of possible activity are training sessions with actors or outings to unusual or glamorous locations. These need to be treated with some caution as not all staff feel happy being asked to do something they have never tried physically. A regular columnist in *Human Resources* magazine suggests saving your money and investing in a pub crawl with a stretch limo!

Perhaps a more acceptable version of the trip to the pub could involve stealing ideas from the pub's own activities in engaging customers. Sports teams and 'pub-style' quizzes are popular with some groups. Both of these provide opportunities for longer-term relationship building within teams and with management and have been dubbed 'social glue' after the trust they are supposed to help foster between individuals and organization. If you are expecting your workforce to join in these activities in their own time, do not put too much emphasis on the work-related messages – keep them subliminal.

EVENTS

Roadshows and other mass face-to-face events have been covered elsewhere in this chapter. Events can also be seen to fit rather well into the corporate glue category but they warrant a section of their own.

There is a whole industry out there dedicated to what is termed incentive or corporate hospitality. Razzmatazz comes to the fore when motivation is regarded as the key driver behind the chosen communication strategy. Due to their expense these are most likely to be favoured for very large gatherings.

They are probably best reserved for grand announcements and the good news end of the scale rather than bad news. However, this category also includes what has been termed 'town halls' – mass meetings of all employees in one location – which could be described as regular fixtures on the corporate diary.

Mary Cowlett writing in *PR Week*, 17 September 2004, highlights how such an event was used to reassure employees at life sciences specialist Amersham shortly after its takeover by what was then GE Medical Systems. The structure was one of celebration and was used to launch the new brand identity.

Geographically dispersed groups that rarely touch base in an office setting can also be reached effectively via this route. Theming the occasion helps to render it something of an event to be remembered alongside the key messages.

ENVIRONMENT

There are of course other ways in which the organization communicates intentionally or otherwise with its employees. The underlying message from the company which fitted its offices out with artificial lawn was unclear, as were the uses to which it was put by its grateful recipients. The Design Council has a meeting area fitted out with a pebble floor.

The Arts have come off the gallery wall and into the office space in a number of initiatives across the country. An artist or something similar in residence has proved a popular way of attracting staff interest and demonstrating the company is more than a money-making machine. Care is needed to ensure these activities do not coincide with redundancies as there may be understandable cynicism and resistance generated.

On a more prosaic level the job titles given to employees can also communicate some rather interesting subliminal messages. 'Marketing evangelist' is a particular favourite of the author.

Perhaps rather more useful to the external community is the opportunity for staff to help the adopted charity of their organization's choice. The LE Group like many others has extensive programmes which work at both local and national levels. These serve a useful double function of linking the organization with the wider community and motivating staff in the process. These schemes can form part of an organization's corporate social responsibility programme and deserve a section to themselves.

CORPORATE SOCIAL RESPONSIBILITY

Corporate social responsibility programmes have obviously been with us in some guise for years but are moving on from nice-to-have to must-have status. Demonstrating that an organization has an impact beyond share-holders underpins this initiative. It is obviously much wider than simply making a donation to the chairman's wife's favourite charity or the odd trip out to the local school.

At a local level, organizations usually pull in their current and future workforce from the surrounding community, so being seen to act properly within it is essential for maintaining the respect of employees.

The most visible and possibly involving way of demonstrating corporate social responsibility to the workforce is by engaging them in working within the community – either locally or in a way that is more appropriate to business interests.

There is a perception that it is the animal and child welfare charities that benefit most from corporate largesse, but as this sector becomes sophisti-cated this is less frequently the case.

Few people would deny that mental health is hardly a cuddly issue, yet emotional health charity, Samaritans, has forged numerous effective partnerships in some rather unexpected places.

A tie-up with insurance giant Royal & SunAlliance has secured the charity funds for brave new projects aimed at young people. But the business itself has found ways of not only getting local employees involved in local branches of the charity but also offering its own facilities to charity volunteers and employees.

It is something of a two-way street as without any pressure, a large proportion of the charity's branches have taken out insurance policies with the company.

Such CSR programmes need to be seen as ongoing activities to overcome any cynicism regarding underlying motives, and to set them apart from the cause-related marketing and sponsorship programmes of yester-year.

There are in fact many ways for businesses to demonstrate a commitment to matters supposedly additional to the bottom line, but those involving employees are likely to bring extra added value. Photogenic activities can provide material for internal communication vehicles reaching a wider audience. They can also be used by the external relations department, but take care to secure permission for use of such images from the host charity. Volunteering programmes appeal not just to not-for-profit organizations but also to public sector bodies including schools and hospitals. Several large city financial institutions have well-established programmes whereby their employees assist with reading and numeracy classes. Older pupils may benefit from mentoring on a one-to-one rather than group basis, which could be designed to help them decide their future career paths or simply provide them with role models. Less potentially labour intensive would be opportunities for public speaking, particularly at school and university careers days.

Employees might prefer getting their hands dirty, and environmental projects provide a great opportunity for group bonding over the shovels. Nature reserves and other conservation projects provide a structured and very real challenge for teams, as do community projects needing a fresh lick of paint.

More senior members of staff can benefit from offering their specialist skills in an advisory as well as a more practical, hands-on approach. Charities frequently have problems in finding treasurers to help balance the books or securing marketing advice. These activities offer the individual with the necessary skills an opportunity to enhance their CV as well as helping the organization plug expertise gaps.

The Media Trust is a charity which offers a range of services including matching media practitioners such as public relations professionals to organizations in need of skills and advice. Alternatively, charity staff can be invited to shadow a commercial counterpart and vice versa in order to experience other ways of working and inject new perspectives.

Local councils and health bodies along with the larger commercial organizations can build their employees' skills by actually seconding them to run a charity or community organization or project. Such schemes are particularly good for middle and more senior managers who are being groomed for higher positions. The recipient organization also benefits from an injection of high-level skills they might not otherwise be able to afford. Banking giant Barclays has found this a great way to refresh employee skills, giving staff renewed enthusiasm and perhaps, just as importantly, a reason to stay. Retention of key staff in the job-is-not-for-life climate is one of the biggest challenges facing employers in all sectors.

Large businesses, including the supermarket giants, are inundated with bids from not-for-profits wishing to be their 'charity of the year'. The most successful partnerships provide scope for the commercial partner's staff to get involved in fundraising activities often of their own design. Dress-down days are a non-time consuming way of involving staff but sponsored runs, walks, beard shaves and the like are ways to amuse as well as enthuse.

Commercial organizations often express envy at the seemingly effortless way their not-for-profit cousins attract such high levels of engagement from their teams. Corporate social responsibility schemes, particularly those making real efforts to engage with local communities, could well help in this respect.

KEY POINTS TO REMEMBER

- Before selecting the media hone the message.
- Segment your audiences and check their media preferences.
- Check timing is right.
- Pick and choose from a media mix rather than concentrating on just one.
- Employees rate face to face highest but keep messages simple and consistent.
- Face-to-face group meetings require supporting material.
- Build in two-way feedback mechanisms.
- Print is easily portable and is a medium of record.
- Keep a balance of news and features in print.
- The moving image is engaging – use it to do just that.
- DVDs offer audience participation.
- Audio cassettes are still good for mobile audiences.
- E-mail and intranet can be hard on the eyes.
- Pare material for screen-based media.
- Text messages are good for news flashes and alerts.
- Quirky gimmicks like board games can engage.
- CSR helps motivate the workforce.

9

Who uses which media for what

The way communication flows around an organization and equally the ways in which it fails to do so should be your first and paramount concern. If you do not pay attention to this area you may as well be shouting down a black hole because that will be the destination for most of your communication efforts.

Organizational culture features in Chapter 4. Here we will look in some detail at the top-down view of communication and in the next chapter will focus on the receiving end.

THE MANAGER'S PERSPECTIVE

Patrick Dunne, Group Communications Director at 3i, appeared to debunk the apparently impressive state of affairs of the all-seeing all-knowing big boss. At least he did in terms of addressing the evidence for strategic top level thinking when he talked to the Internal Communication Alliance in spring 2003. Referring in particular to the boards of relatively new companies, he warned that some executive directors were none too aware of how they were perceived by their staff and consequently put a low priority on internal communication. He suggests seizing the chance to talk to the boss at an unplanned opportunity – in the back of a cab perhaps.

At some level managers have to choose a method or combination of methods for delivering their messages. They are likely to be picking from a communication continuum which runs from the personal right through to the impersonal. The personal focuses on face-to-face, one-to-one communication – the conversation between two individuals, and to which might be added small and larger group discussions and briefings. At the other end of the spectrum lie the impersonal all-encompassing publications and broadcasts (both aural and visual).

Alexander, Penley and Jernigan (1991) rank face-to-face, telephone, meetings, notes, memos and group memos in descending order of 'media richness', or the personal, interactive feel of the communication. As organizations grow they are presumed to move closer to the midpoint of the continuum and away from the more personal approach.

Movement along the continuum highlights some of the perceived weaknesses of the face-to-face approach which may centre on sustaining credibility over time. Daft, Lengel and Trevino, quoted by Yates and Orlikowski (1992), suggest that written media gets attention, while the telephone is deemed as urgent and requiring action. They have not slotted e-mail into the calculation but it combines characteristics from both telephone and print and has as good as replaced the memo.

At the mass media or impersonal end of the communications spectrum, the very nature of it suggests a lack of possibility for interaction and feedback. A degree of formality is achieved by what is arguably a uniform approach. There are advantages – everyone gets the same message, hence consistency in the case of printed and video, DVD or audio cassette-based communication and can consume them in their own time. Face-to-face communication on a one-to-several or one-to-many basis does not give much scope for absorption and reflection but allows for checking and feedback.

The argument has to be whether or not the personal and impersonal approaches are necessarily mutually exclusive. Perhaps it could be argued that there is a middle terrain opened up by technology.

TOP DOWN – BUT WHAT ABOUT THE WORKERS?

The conventional model of communication favoured by many organizations will be top-down. It would be naive to suppose otherwise. There will always be a need for senior management to give guidance on the direction in which it wants the organization and its constituent teams to head. But top management should also be paying attention to and encouraging lateral communication which by virtue of its nature criss-crosses the organization and from which fresh perspectives may come. Just as hard is encouraging a true upward flow of communication from the front line to the boardroom.

With 23,000 employees, Customs and Excise centralized the communication function in London to cut through layers of bureaucracy which had been muffling the message. A multitude of largely print-based media has been replaced with a variety of channels. Internal communication is no longer seen as an add-on but as an intrinsic part of the organization's business strategy. Centralized advisers mean the 'silo effect' can be circumnavigated. Many organizations featuring more than one profession will use a metaphor for organizational blockages in terms of communication which lends itself to chimneys. Apparently they are all operating quite separately and sending out their own plumes of smoke.

Customs and Excise has dubbed the behaviour they want to see embedded as 'active management'. The emphasis is on open and transparent communication, effective leadership, building effective teams, a sense of being personally accountable, focusing on outcome not process, matching service to customer needs and making good use of available technology.

Tackling such major change does, however, need the complete commitment of the top team, otherwise efforts will come to nought or could prove counterproductive.

One local authority did not have time on its side in the mid-1990s when it needed to change the way in which its front-line staff were delivering services to the public. The old-style approach had something of the bureaucracy about it with the emphasis very much on the function performed rather than on the unfortunate person on the receiving end of its beneficent gestures. It could take literally weeks to carry out anything more than a simple repair.

Without the possibility of a large training budget the textbook approach to organizational development had to be abandoned. Instead the former functional heads were all asked individually what it was they most needed in order to do their job.

Rather depressingly they all wanted a new filing system, and they all wanted it to have very specific qualities. Needless to say there were as many versions of this system as there were people wanting to use it.

The solution came from designing the filing system to focus on the client group rather than the specialist skill. Effectively the filing system was used in a purely symbolic sense. Making the individuals look at their work from a different angle achieved a team focus in a very short period of time.

This example shows new ways in which the internal communicator can assist in the reshaping of the organization by helping break down old mindsets. Effectively this is culture change or change management.

ENSURING SOMEONE IS LISTENING

Obviously communicating like mad is all very well, but how can the professional communicator possibly be sure anyone is actually paying attention? The most brilliant publication and internal website will be absolutely worthless if there is nobody actually reading or keying into them.

Building in feedback mechanisms not only provides the communicator with the opportunity to check if there is anybody out there; it also offers up a chance of interactivity. Many of the media channels offered can, if not designed appropriately, encourage a degree of passivity on the part of the recipient.

Adding the opportunity to engage and express opinion opens up a virtuous circle of communication, outlined by Pamela Mounter in Anne Gregory's *Public Relations in Practice* (2004) as illustrated in Figure 9.1 below. Ideas and suggestions that are fed back into the system help keep the communication process flowing. In conversational modes of communication (face to face) this can be done by constantly checking for understanding. In mediated communication (publications, websites, etc) other slightly more sophisticated techniques are required. These can be heavily disguised in the form of competitions and polls. But remember the roadblocks may be higher up the organization than you might have imagined.

Figure 9.1 *Virtuous circle of communication – building in feedback loops improves all-round communication*

UNBLOCKING THE BLOCKAGES

This is where an effective internal communicator can be of service to all layers of an organization in taking temperature checks throughout on a regular basis and alerting senior management to problem areas well in advance. This is similar in role to that of the model external communicator feeding back critical issues arising from the competition and other aspects of the outside world.

The potential for distortion somewhere between the top level and the front line has been brought out by the author's case studies on a number of occasions. A particularly good example is presented by Bristol and West Building Society which had introduced monthly team briefing sessions back in 1992. It felt that face-to-face communication was a good method for encouraging employees to achieve specific goals.

Although well received to start with, satisfaction with the system had declined over time. Particular concerns were raised in specific regions, suggesting that the problem was not necessarily rooted in the actual selection of channel but in the way in which it was being delivered on the ground.

The situation had been complicated still further by the society's move to demutualize in order to become a mortgage bank. Quite a lot of employees did not really understand what lay ahead and how things might have to be done differently.

When the alarm bells rang, the society called in the MCA consultancy to identify first the problem and then the solution. Under the old system the emphasis had been on the manager talking and the employees listening; there appeared to be plenty of scope for some managers to put their own 'spin' on issues.

Research by the consultancy highlighted these issues. The 'Team Listening' programme changed the focus from the manager's contribution to everyone's. Employees were sent a briefing document in advance of the meeting to enable them to contribute rather than simply listen.

The new system was so well received that it was rolled out across the organization. The in-house communication team was equipped with the skills to deliver the programme more widely and to continue to fine tune it as organizational and employee needs changed.

The panel below lists some typical blocks to communication.

MEDIA OR SYMBOL?

In some sectors the choice of media can be powered by symbolic as well as or instead of more practical considerations.

BLOCKS TO COMMUNICATION

- age;
- gender;
- disability;
- culture (religion);
- channel distortions;
- overactive grapevine;
- previous history of organization;
- distrust in management;
- too much of the same old thing;
- regional differences.

Symbolism can be seen at work in companies which encourage a 'management by walking about' culture and require top management to be seen either with an open door or the willingness to get their hands dirty on the shop floor.

Consultant Bill Quirke (2002) says that communication should not simply tell, but should also involve explanation as the workforce wants to be perceived as adult enough to understand what is being asked of them.

Channels which allow for some interaction are likely to prove the most successful and do not necessarily have to be the most high-tech. *BUPA News* and the *John Lewis Gazette*, both print publications, amply demonstrate that it is possible to convert seemingly one-way vehicles to take two-way traffic. Feedback may not be immediate but time for reflection may result in a better quality of response.

What probably drives most top management decisions in terms of channel is very similar to what motivates them in the wider business sense. Will the vehicle selected do the job for the least money and the greatest return?

The Work Foundation has conducted much research into internal communication and its report on the subject published in 2002 shows management regarding team briefings as the most effective channel (60 per cent). E-mail is close behind at 59 per cent and intranet is at 38 per cent. This last should give pause for thought as this would seem to imply it should be used in a support capacity rather than provide the main communication platform. Alternatively it could just be indicative of how far the medium had spread at the time of the survey.

However, these overlook the most prevalent and therefore arguably the most important communication channel of them all – the grapevine. No organization has ever been able to outlaw gossip, so why not go with the flow? It at least provides another outlet for information.

THE INVISIBLE WEB

The average organizational communication chart looks rather like a road map which has been designed to show only the motorways and A roads, omitting the supposedly minor B, C and unclassified roads. You may be able to reach your destination with this map but you need to be aware of the deceptively minor routes – the grapevine.

Attempts to block the grapevine – by strenuous monitoring of e-mails, the reintroduction of the tea lady (no more coffee machine chats), or ever stricter rules on working practice will make little difference.

On a positive note, informal channels can also be described as lateral ones – these are criss-cross routes or shortcuts that individuals use to ensure they can do their job. Much of the chat may seem just that, but it can aid the smooth flow of information that needs to get through. The best course of action is to learn to use informal channels, either by tuning in to find out what is being said or to transmit your messages.

Organizations across the sectors are using a variety of distinctly 'gossipy' techniques to draw attention to important messages. IBM alerts its car-bound salespeople to the arrival of regular communication of a substantial nature via text messaging. Sue Ryder Care flags up news on its intranet. North Tees and Hartlepool NHS Trust has dubbed its confidential phone line the 'rumour line' in a bid to get people to sort out problems without necessarily having to resort to whistle-blowing when the traditional line management route fails. There are a variety of stages en route to true knowledge management or sharing of information across an organization.

But knowledge management takes a great deal of effort. LE Group has 3,000 pages of information on its intranet. Finding your way round that scale of operation could become even more daunting than circumnavigating a huge corporate manual in printed form without effective signposting.

Humour has been used by IBM in a bid to encourage staff to personalize their own workspace so the information they receive is the information they need. Even though this is by its very nature a high-technology company, it took a lot of effort to get employees to take advantage of a mechanism designed to make life easier for them. A quirky advertisement was transmitted to overcome initial inertia.

Another more human way of encouraging cross-organizational communication is to create a working environment where employees can meet informally and spark ideas. Back to the water cooler anyone?

However, a more formal way of looking at this is to increase the number of 'dotted line' connections that people have across an organization. Many of those talked to in the course of producing this book have direct reporting lines but also dotted-line links with other departments which are most likely to include human resources. These lines are also formal recognition that most people need to communicate in more than one direction.

KEY POINTS TO REMEMBER

- Top-down communication continues to prevail.
- Layers of bureaucracy can stifle messages.
- Centralizing communication can cut the silo effect but replace this with 'us and them'.
- Variety is the spice of life in terms of channels.
- Interactivity should be built into media to overcome passivity.
- Take regular soundings from the workforce to spot blockages and breakdowns.
- Media selected can have symbolic properties not immediately obvious.
- Recognize and use the grapevine judiciously.
- Build in opportunities for cross-organization communication via the organizational chart.

10

The receiving end

STAFF PERCEPTIONS

Here the spotlight is turned on the other end of the communication transaction – the receiving end, the audience, the public, your reader, listener, viewer and whatever you call the person manipulating their mouse around the intranet.

The title of this section should in fact go against the grain of all the rhetoric on involvement, engagement and interactivity that has gone before, and is the mantra of the in-house communication specialist. However, it probably more closely reflects the reality of life on the front line or wherever the chosen target is located.

It can be hard to gain access to those 'on the receiving end', or to their true views. Much of what is available is likely to be anecdotal although the now strong commitment by organizations to measurement and evaluation suggests this will not always be the case.

In-house people and consultants of a certain seniority have been keen to emphasize the need to ensure whatever media you select should be able to stand up against the competition from the high street newsagent. Concern about glossy values, certainly in publications produced in the public and not-for-profit sectors, can backfire as individuals can read something extra into your motives for the chosen approach. They could perceive this as a misuse of funds or a way of hiding what they believe to be bad news.

Some years ago in the health service the author was responsible for editing a six-page newsletter aimed purely at employees. It was black and white and used photography imaginatively. It also included a mix of 'business' news and more feature-based material. But these were the days of the purchaser–provider split with hospitals supposedly 'selling' themselves to local family doctors and the like.

A decision was taken at senior managerial level to go for a full-colour tabloid glossy. There was still not much of a budget, but this publication had to do something most communicators would counsel against – mixing up internal and external audiences. Actually it was a great success with both the external group and employees who felt valued as a result of receiving a publication with far higher production values than previously. They were often to be seen reading it and proffered their news for inclusion. It lasted until the subsequent health service reorganization.

IS THERE ANYBODY THERE?

One way to find out whether your publication is hitting the mark is to include a Readers' Letters column which allows full-blown criticism of both the publication itself and the wider management. Light touch paper, stand back and wait. But be prepared for a deafening silence. People often cannot be bothered to respond, do not have the time or are too afraid of possible consequences.

For a refresher course on how to get your audience tuning in, just look at what is happening in the mass media equivalent and pinch the ideas for yourself. Seeboard rather neatly got its workers firmly behind the drive to rebrand the organization and demonstrate its focus on creating value. It staged auditions for them to appear in advertisements which in turn promoted the brand. Fans of numerous talent-based programmes entered in their droves.

Employees were also filmed in situ at work for a video which again proved a huge motivator and helped other groups understand their colleagues' jobs. The bottom line demonstrated the approach worked, as customer attrition went down substantially and more employees stayed in their jobs – not necessarily the industry norm.

Possibly the same kind of people would respond to polls on the intranet as a light-hearted way of gaining not only interaction but also feedback. It does, however, pay to ask formally for reader, listener or viewer views in a structured way from time to time – annually is probably sufficient. Readership surveys or the broadcast equivalents will draw out views on content and design. (Evaluation is covered more fully in Chapter 20.)

INVOLVEMENT THE KEY

One organization which clearly understands that the real power in its hierarchical organization chart is not at the pinnacle of the triangle but in its base is the Church of England. Alexander Nicoll is the first Head of Internal Communications appointed by the Church's version of the Cabinet Office, the Archbishops' Council.

The Church came to internal communications as an identifiable function rather late, having taken a decision in council in 1998 that it was needed. Attempting the 'megaphone' approach to communication was felt unlikely to work. Parishes on the ground act rather like the regional or local branches of some organizations; they can take it or leave it – whatever it is.

'The way to describe the role is to imagine us as in a maze. You cannot easily re-route the maze but you can trim the hedges so those in the maze can be more aware of each other. Operational and other benefits accrue to all, wherever we work for the Church as a result', Alexander Nicoll said.

Feedback is probably one of the most important features which can be built into a communication vehicle in terms of both the health of the organization and of the 'publication' itself. Intranets are no exception and taking a leaf out of a commercial website will do no harm.

One of the earlier adopters of the intranet was PHH Europe which first explored the subject in 1997 but had to leave it on the proverbial backburner until 2000, as a meeting of the then Internal Communications Group heard.

Having brought employees up to speed on intranet use, a chatline was installed. There were no holds barred, according to Employee Communications Manager Rosie Mowatt. Favoured topics included car parking and smoking. Managers were encouraged to provide feedback and this had an effect on policy making.

One thing learnt in commissioning the site was that designers would have got carried away with the gimmicks at the expense of content if given free rein. What was more important was to include useful things which not only got the job done but made life easier – like including menus for the canteen. Alongside the more serious learning and development tools there was also a barter board allowing employees to put up 'small ads'. These devices encourage interaction and informal feedback.

LAST ON THE BANDWAGON?

Those who have abandoned print for intranet-based communication may find they have trouble engaging older workers or individuals for whom English is not their first language. Providing training in computer skills does not necessarily mean even relatively senior people will actually go online.

Being aware and sympathetic of the true abilities of your publics is crucial if you do not want to be communicating into a black hole. Ease of access to technology as part of the daily workload will determine whether employees will make the extra effort to access intranets.

This is also something to remember when the latest must-have gadget hits the marketplace. Text messaging at the time of going to press was obviously the rage among younger members of staff, but it may not prove quite so popular for those with arthritic thumbs and bifocal spectacles.

Also at the time of writing, 3G phones were being adopted introducing pictures to a phone near you. Although entertainment value can be gauged, the jury is still out on practicality. Disability discrimination legislation requires you to consider how to make your publications, intranets and roadshows accessible to all.

GIVE THEM WHAT THEY NEED TO DO THE JOB

At the end of the day the major purpose of internal communication is to help people do their job. Consultancy Redhouse Lane has done this by producing online and print-version guides to help employees in the National Health Service do their daily jobs much more effectively.

The format in this case is an important part of the ingredients, which include the information employees need in a handy format that is easily accessible. The printed version comes in pocket-sized wipe-clean booklets, just the thing for on the ward. The online version has been designed to ensure it can be transported across to other formats whenever the computer systems are changed. Elsewhere in the health service informal online chatlines have been established to provide a more friendly way for nurses to update their skills by exchanging tips and problems with their peers across the profession.

But John Arlidge of the *Observer* (2 March 2002) quoted in a 2002 issue of the Relationship Foundation newsletter warns that we are in danger of e-mailing more than we talk. Apparently the average office bound worker spends three hours a day sending and receiving around 150 e-mails. Remember those health and safety exhortations to get away from the computer screen? Perhaps a communications mix would make that more of a possibility.

A paper by Nathan and Doyle (2002) of the then Industrial Society (now the Work Foundation) sketches out the communicative properties of the physical office or other workspace and how they have an impact on the individual and their interaction with colleagues. Office design can also have an effect on channels of communication, particularly if the selected channels require free association between individuals and there is a filing cabinet in the way!

THE IN-HOUSE LANGUAGE

A related matter is that of in-house language. Many professions and for that matter organizations have their own private language which can serve to exclude those not in the know.

There is a difference between jargon and private language. Jargon usually refers to precise terminology which is employed by individuals experienced in their field – medicine and science come to mind. But injudicious use of such language to the wrong audience can be quite alienating.

Private language, however, refers more particularly to an organization's shorthand. This may have its uses but again will exclude some people. There is a danger that if an internal communicator identifies too closely with the organization they may forget that the language used means nothing to those outside the inner circle. The quick way to find out is to question a newcomer not only to the organization but to the sphere of work.

UPWARDS COMMUNICATION

More and more attention is now being paid to how communication is channelled back up an organization from the front line. Attitude surveys are now being seen as a vital way of getting the voice of the employee heard.

Voice of the Employee is the title of Cable & Wireless's regular programme, which mirrors its rather more established Voice of the Customer survey. Employees are polled anonymously to seek their views on key areas of their working life, from their relationship with their manager, to their perception of the company's customer service. These can then be cross-tabulated against customer feedback to establish just how well they match up, providing another form of evaluation.

As proof that management really does take on board comments made, employees in one office expressed strong objections to their working environment. The comments were consistent enough for the company to actually relocate their office – which must have been a powerful vindication of feedback and ultimately motivator as employees saw that their comments were not only acknowledged but also dealt with.

Allied Irish Bank discovered some years ago that internal communication worked well downwards, but that upward communication was not effective. It decided to make its employee survey a more regular feature but it also looked at what it considered as less formal channels of communication. Head of Staff Communications Grace Perrott actually uses the phrase 'formalized grapevine'.

A lot of input and support is required for employee consultation groups which act as the listening ears of the organization. They meet the general management every six weeks to discuss issues and share ideas. Much effort was put in to ensure the groups did not simply become complaints panels. They need the support of the top management, otherwise they will not maintain their credibility on the shop floor. The managers on the receiving end have to commit to feed back their responses and reports are made on at least a quarterly basis.

Key communication issues would appear to be securing support from top management, whatever communication vehicles and programmes are selected, and investing the money, the time and the people into these vehicles in order to build in a sounding-board element which is taken seriously.

CONCLUSIONS TO BE DRAWN

The employee population is one public that organizations ignore at their own risk.

Although management tends to see the media as the most important audience, the far more critical group is employees. External audiences judge organizations to some extent on the way they treat their employees, while inside the organization a dedication to commitment and common purpose will boost corporate self-esteem. So all those *Sunday Times* supplements on the best employers to work for may well be onto something.

There has been a tendency among companies and communicators to overlook the fact that many employees are now shareholders in their own right. Transmitting conflicting messages to different audiences will no longer work – if it ever did. The entire senior management team should become the focus of communication training by the communications specialists.

The UK's Co-operative Bank is quoted as having a distinctive stakeholder ethos which has been running since the mid-1990s. In addition to taking on board the needs of shareholders and customers, the bank also involves seven other partner groups in its activities. These include staff, suppliers, local communities, national and international societies and past and future generations of co-operators. The proof of the pudding – profits have doubled and it features in the *Sunday Times* best employers list. The conclusion of the article is that communicators should not only listen to those who shout loudest, but also pay attention to the quieter stakeholders, especially employees.

So how do you tackle information overload? The panel below provides some pointers; see also Chapter 19 for e-mail etiquette.

TACKLING INFORMATION OVERLOAD

- Train the communicators – do they need to say it at all?
- Train those on the receiving end on using technology.
- Do not restrict all communication to one channel – vary it.
- Establish realistic response times.
- Encourage staff to apply a clear electronic in-tray policy.
- Label missives clearly to help prioritization.
- Agree e-mail protocols.
- Never press 'reply all'.
- Ban e-mail once a week!

Last words go to John Smythe, writing in the *Smythe Dorward Lambert Review* of the profession back in 1995: 'We can now deliver more information via e-mail, satellite TV, print, multimedia and the internet than most people can make sense of. And that's what employees are saying to all of us; information pollution and overload are the greatest barriers to understanding.'

KEY POINTS TO REMEMBER

- Employee perceptions sometimes override reality – glossy could equal profligacy to them.
- Feedback mechanisms do not have to be sophisticated – try letters pages, quick polls on intranet and text.
- Keep corporate aspirations for the media channel simple to avoid disappointment at board level.
- Content is king – ensure it is useful to the audience.
- Provide support for formalized feedback channels to help the workforce to use them.

11

Communicating with special groups

In the sections that follow we specifically deal with disabled people, and those of different cultural and racial backgrounds, age, gender and sexual orientation. We will also look at how other employees may react and how to overcome any feelings of exclusion. Other sections include work teams working away from base and the motivation of volunteers. Chapter 12 will deal in particular with communicating across globally dispersed communities.

Issues you may well have to start considering include dealing with different cultures and nationalities whether they be working within your physical environment or on their home turf, wherever that might be.

Certain industries and certain companies at a particular stage of their development may be recruiting younger staff who are likely to have very different media preferences from older members of the team.

Your business may require you to hire people who do not turn up for work in the conventional office-bound sense but work at one remove from you, either at home or on the road, rarely touching base. Some may work on your premises but only at set times. The permutations are endless.

In these days of diversity you are increasingly legally obliged to take account of the specific needs of different racial and religious groups. Companies also need to take account of the 'pink pound'. Gay and lesbian workers are also covered by anti-discrimination laws.

Laws also apply to workers with disabilities and these will not just apply to those with obvious physical problems, but to those with mental health and learning disabilities too.

Not-for-profit sector organizations and some public sector examples such as hospitals can rely heavily on workers who do not get paid. Getting them to turn up and do what you want on a consistent and regular basis is particularly challenging.

Increasingly, very tiny organizations are going to have to give a bit more thought to their communication processes, particularly in these days of litigation at the drop of a hat.

Giving all due consideration to the above-mentioned fine-tuning of the generic structures, processes and products, the organization should benefit not just from a reduced legal bill, but from a more committed workforce that will reflect its customer base and the community in which it is based. So this is not just a 'nice to have', but a business imperative.

TAPPING INTO CULTURAL DIVERSITY

In little more than half a century the face of Britain has changed out of all recognition and this is just as true of the workforce as it is the general population. English is unlikely to be the first language of a great number of individuals across the country.

Many of them will celebrate different religious holidays, and perhaps have a completely different date for the start of their calendar year. During the working day they may need to stop work to pray or carry out other faith-related duties.

Not only do managements have to take note of these very different needs, they will also have to manage the potential resentments and raised expectations of the rest of the workforce.

When planning roadshows, conferences and other briefing sessions it would pay to ensure that programmes have frequent breaks designed into them. Concentration spans are notoriously shorter than management reckon, so these breaks need to be sufficient to allow those carrying out religious activities to have enough time to get fed and watered too!

Recently introduced legislation means that if special arrangements are made for one group, their equivalent must be made available to other religious groups within the workforce. There may be something to be learnt from the NHS where the chaplaincy service in many large hospitals is often staffed by practitioners from a number of faiths.

When considering the content of publications (print or internet based) and broadcast you could use cultural diversity as an opportunity to share different perspectives with the whole workforce. Bearing in mind that

English may not be the prime language of all, it is worth stripping copy of jokes, idiomatic phrases and homespun wisdom because they may not be understood. Younger people generally may find references to long-gone practices quite incomprehensible.

You may feel that producing separate translations would be very costly. A cheaper option would be to compile a list of individuals willing to interpret or translate into their own language. Incorporated into publications, boxed panels could include a simple phrase in many available languages directing employees to the interpreter service. This could also be a valuable added extra for customers or service users.

People with limited English find newsprint especially hard to read. The solution: select better-quality paper, use an easy-to-read typeface (serif like Times Roman) in a reasonable size, at least 12 pt.

In some cultural groups it may prove difficult to reach women in particular, or older groups. They may be effectively approached by individuals recognized as elders or as well informed: they usually turn out to be the ones with a rather better grasp of English. Women from certain cultural or faith backgrounds will feel more comfortable embarking on an activity in the company of others like themselves.

The 2001 Census shows 7.9 per cent of the population is classified as non-white, and that by 2010 30 per cent of city populations will come from ethnic communities. Most people working in the UK industry are in fact white and British. A *PR Week* survey published in September 2003 shows just 4 per cent of all PR account managers in the UK come from an ethnic background.

Anne Gregory, Professor of Public Relations at Leeds Metropolitan University, says: 'As an industry and as a professional association, we need to draw on the expertise of all areas of society. There's no question that we need the insight of a diverse community and it's not about being PC. The approach needs to be holistic – if not, we're missing the richness of our society' (*Profile* magazine, Issue 42, March/April 2004 pp 14–15).

THE DIFFERENTLY ABLED

Stiff financial penalties should persuade organizations, large or small, to make 'reasonable' adjustments to render premises and services accessible. Naming and shaming is part of the Disability Rights Commission's armoury, so be warned.

Areas of concern can focus on hearing, sight, mobility (not just feet but hands), voice and conditions invisible to the naked eye. This latter could relate to mobility if it concerns spinal difficulties, mental health, learning disabilities and neurological conditions.

Computers can now be provided with large screens similar to those popular with graphic designers; they can also offer very large and easy-to-read typefaces, be voice activated and have a sound feature – all of which will especially help with sight issues. Braille could well be appropriate. Alternatively, taped publications work very well and these can be extended to a car-bound workforce.

Organizations like Action for Blind People can give sound advice on the size of typeface you should use in any publication for people with reading problems – and you would probably also take care of the more senior lobby too.

Publication design should take on board the fact that a large percentage of the population wears some form of glasses and may find the current trend for small, elegant but thin typefaces puts them off reading. A similar complaint can be levelled at many designers of overheads for presentations. Short-sighted people have particular problems with too much information in too small a print.

People with hearing difficulties have a range of options open to them which come into play in the face-to-face arena. Induction loops are an unobtrusive way of ensuring everything can be heard. It is, however, essential to ensure all mobile phones are switched off as they can interfere with the functioning of the loop and for that matter any computerized presentation system too.

Many individuals who are hard of hearing may prefer sign language, and interpreters can be incorporated into meeting plans. Here it is wise for those needing the service and those providing it to be in close proximity to each other as sight lines are all important. In one-to-ones and smaller group meetings the speaker should make sure they face the individual(s) con-cerned as many of them can lip-read or use lip-reading to reinforce hearing aids.

Intranets as well as external websites can be adapted to meet access requirements. However, these adaptations can serve to slow down workers without these conditions. More than one version of an internal website may be necessary to overcome this, and any potential resentments that may arise in the wider workforce. Again the relevant charities in the field are a good source of advice and many earn some of their necessary funding from such consultancy.

Make allowances too for employees in wheelchairs or with mobility issues. Meeting spaces should be designed to allow for wheelchairs to be manoeuvred into position; wide aisles and perhaps space at the front of an auditorium will help meet these requirements.

Mental health and learning disability issues are particularly challenging as these problems are largely invisible to the untrained eye. The internal communicator needs to ensure that the content of publications, intranets, videos and the like does not inadvertently compound existing prejudices.

There are charities which campaign to rid the mass media of the kind of language which can only underline alienation. 'Going nuts for May' could seem an innocent headline but is likely to attract criticism.

When setting up editorial boards and consultative panels involving staff groups, you can address many of the above issues by the inclusion of individuals who have a personal knowledge of specific issues – age, culture, disability, etc. More than one appointee would go some way to overcoming possible accusations of tokenism.

AGE, GENDER AND SEXUAL ORIENTATION

It comes to us all in time – age, that is. With discrimination legislation being beefed up to include older people you can expect more than a sprinkling of grey in the workforce in future. Many of the issues underlined in the previous section on disability may also apply to at least some older members of the workforce, but it is important not to forge a direct link between the two in the wider population's minds. However, older employees may well appreciate adjustments for sight, hearing and mobility to varying degrees.

When it comes to gender – we all have one. The professional communicator should take care not to make assumptions about either gender or age. Football may have seemed a male preserve for many years, but now members of Girlguiding UK are listing it as one of their favourite sports to try, not just to watch.

Younger team members can also feel discriminated against. Rather more positively, they can be technically very literate, having grown up with computer games at their fingertips. But a recent trend to watch is the rise of the silver surfer – the older internet fan. When designing programmes it is worth establishing actual ability, needs and interests and this can be done unobtrusively through surveys.

If you have a relatively young team, up-to-the-minute technologically driven activities may well be the key. Before deciding to go down the publication route it would be useful to establish whether the proposed recipients even read such a thing as a newspaper on a daily or weekly basis. Finding out what kind of publication does meet favour will help determine the format to adopt.

Sexual orientation is a recent addition to the list of issues to be handled sensitively. Do not make the assumption that all your colleagues are heterosexual marrieds. Careful balance in presentation of information over time should ensure all shades of opinion and choice are catered for. Scrupulously check copy and images for anything which may inadvertently or otherwise offend.

WORKING FROM HOME OR OUT ON THE ROAD

Engineers, sales forces and professionals in general are increasingly likely not to be working from one fixed office. Keeping them in the communications loop can be an added complication in day-to-day communication.

They face isolation if they do not have much social contact with their colleagues. The implication for the communicator is that they need more information not less, and special efforts need to be made to keep them aware of the wider team. This can be done through social events but it is important not to consume too much of what they might regard as their personal time to do this.

Those working literally on their own will forge their own networks and these may not include either line managers or colleagues. Their most obvious links could well be with competitors in similar situations and this could prove difficult to handle. Informal grapevines may spring up and rumours may be particularly hard to suppress at a distance. Regular meetings will help to balance this tendency, but more positively these individuals could bring fresh perspectives to issues concerning others.

AA hits the road

The AA's road patrols very rarely come into an office, so need to be communicated with very energetically to keep them informed not only of company matters but also of industry developments that will have an impact on their jobs.

Line managers do pull the teams together for team briefing sessions but these can easily be disrupted by operational requirements. Print materials are backed up with audio tapes and in time these are likely to be replaced by CD ROMs and downloadable material as the mobile technology becomes more widely available. The senior management team gets out and about on a weekly basis to meet up with teams to understand their issues and views.

Something approximating to two-way communication is offered by a phone-in service that allows patrols to contribute their comments and views and share tips they have picked up that might be useful for the rest of their colleagues. Many of these are incorporated in the regular tape-based magazine programmes.

Patrols are not the only remote team members that the AA needs to keep in the loop. The company is able to call on a network of homeworkers who are equipped to take calls from their members, which is particularly useful in times of peak workload. Here face-to-face communication is regarded as important and supervisors get out to visit their employees regularly.

A particular issue for both groups is for the communication practitioners to find ways to help them feel part of a team, even if they never really see the other members. A mix of motivational activities such as awards and good quality information is regarded as critical.

IBM offers choice

Naturally IBM is strong on intranet but it is not always the practical option for its dispersed sales team. Internal Communications Consultancy Manager Sophie Austin obviously has to think of other ways to keep them in touch and actively involved.

Each quarter some 15 speakers are lined up for a recorded conference call which is then 'promoted' to the employees via text messaging. The sales force has a seven-day period to phone in.

It is mandatory to listen to the chief executive's message but then there is an option to choose from the menu of other speakers. To encourage feedback, employees can use their keypad to vote for their favourite speakers. At the centre the communications team gets to know how many phoned in and who they listened to, and how they rated them. With the company's external message being e-business on demand there is a corresponding internal thrust to 'communications on demand'.

THE UNPAID HEROES

Most of Britain's charities run purely on the goodwill of an army of unpaid volunteers. There is no big stick that can be waved in terms of a cut in salary if they do not deliver. Any attempt at coercion is more than likely to result in a downing of tools, probably for good.

Many charities which do have paid staff teams still rely heavily on extensive networks of volunteers to enable them to provide a wide range of services and in some cases to simply staff the office.

With the growing professionalization of the not-for-profit sector, more and more structures are being put in place to support the unpaid crew. Particular attention has to be given to communicating with volunteers in a way that is appropriate to their role.

Large organizations like the Red Cross will have very diverse audiences with which to communicate. Trustees are likely to be busy people, often with impressive jobs elsewhere; they also happen to be the equivalent to the board of directors. In support of the decision-making aspects of their role they need to be included in any communications drive that the organization is planning, be it internal or external.

Fundraising committees often resemble special project teams from the business world more than anything else, and could well include celebrities and VIPs in their number. Again respect for their time and commitment needs to be demonstrated. Publications either dedicated to this group or for wider audiences are useful and events work well.

Keeping services, shops and branch activities going will be a very diverse group of individuals who probably have nothing more in common than the community in which they live or the cause they choose to serve (but not necessarily both). Nowadays all these groups are likely to include very diverse sections of the community.

How you communicate with them will also need to take account of the level of expense that might be involved. A scrappy piece of paper will demonstrate lack of respect, but a full-colour brochure, unless someone else is clearly picking up the tab, could suggest a spendthrift attitude.

Face-to-face activities like conferences and roadshows work well for regionally dispersed supporters, as do discussion fora on the internet. Inclusion in decision making is essential: without their buy-in, activities such as corporate identity makeovers could fail.

The box below gives a few pointers on how to get the best from volunteers. Produced by a real-life volunteer, it can be applied to communication vehicles but also to making best use of such individuals in the work of the communications department itself.

GOLDEN RULES FOR WORKING WITH VOLUNTEERS

Pam Freeman, herself a trustee for several organizations including the UK Federation of Smaller Mental Health Agencies, came up with the following rules for happy volunteers.

- Tell them all there is to know about the organization and their role.
- Give them a trial run to make sure they are as happy as you are.
- Match them to jobs where they can use their full skill mix.
- Treating them too much like staff makes them feel resentful.
- Give them respect and respect their wealth of experience and skills.
- Consider health and safety issues and proper insurance.
- Volunteers give time not money; reimburse their expense.

As the former chief executive of a charity, the author knows it is also a good idea to construct activity in such a way that it provides volunteers with fresh experience and new skills that they can use elsewhere. But recognition for the effort made seems to be the real reward for many.

A 2004 study involving the Salvation Army suggests that volunteers may need to be given something more than the usual warm glow of gratitude, and skills development may enhance their employability. Transferring your own communications skills, particularly with special groups like the media, can be highly prized as Pamela Mounter found when working with the Red Cross many years ago. At least one volunteer who attended the media training workshop went on to a career in radio.

MICRO-ORGANIZATIONS

The bulk of organizations in Britain are tiny. Managing relationships in very small groups can be particularly challenging as there may be as many viewpoints as there are people. In larger organizations it is often possible to find alternative routes to achieving a goal when obstreperous individuals throw up obstacles. Instead of opting for confrontation the communicator, like the line manager, should seek to establish the true reasons for problems which may have nothing to do with the workplace.

An unobtrusive way of achieving this is demonstrated by legal firm Eversheds' Copenhagen office. Numbers are manageable enough to allow them to eat lunch together, providing an informal environment to discuss issues. Not everyone will want to share lunch every day but on a weekly basis this can provide a safe environment for matters of concern to be aired and settled.

CONCLUSIONS

When planning your communications programme it is worth dissecting your audience just to see who they are as individuals. Are they old, young, male, female, predominantly British (whatever that means)? Are they gay, transgender, with families? Balancing the needs of the organization with a healthy respect for the privacy of these same individuals is a tall order.

Incorporating the needs of the various interest groups which your staff might represent can prove expensive in the short term. However, if you are seen to treat employees well and with respect, your corporate reputation can only grow in stature. Diversity should also be seen as an opportunity to tap into a far richer range of points of view.

KEY POINTS TO REMEMBER

- Be prepared to segment your audience along a range of less obvious permutations – age, gender, race, disability, etc.
- Take into account the feelings of all sections of the workforce – look particularly for resentment.
- Cultural diversity could be seen as an opportunity rather than an extra burden on resources.
- Consider quality of paper, size of typeface, use of colour when communicating with audiences with disabilities or from a different cultural background.
- Interpreters are useful in group meetings for people with hearing difficulties but also those who may not speak good English.
- Dispersed teams need a multitude of media choices to ensure their communication needs are met.

12

The globally dispersed workforce

Multinationals will often have to communicate across the globe with dispersed workers and teams. Smaller operators including many communication consultancies work in alliances and partnerships in different markets and they too will also need to pay particular attention to detail. You may also have to combat the NIH or 'not invented here' syndrome, where material produced in one country is deemed unacceptable elsewhere. There is also the rare possibility that expatriates may have gone native, which produces challenges of its own.

Anyway you will need to consider whether or not to translate materials for different markets. As a useful rule of thumb, even if you have A level German you are probably not the best person for translating material into that language for dissemination among native readers or speakers. No matter how good your grasp of the idiosyncrasies of a language, you will never get it quite as on target as someone living in the country at the given moment.

Even where it is presumed that English is spoken, as in America, watch for the cultural minefield. It may even be necessary to translate British-produced material for that audience and vice versa. As with external communication it pays to get people you trust from within the target communities to check your approach as well as the detail to make sure you have got it right. A look at commercial advertising down the years demonstrates how easy it is to get it horribly and expensively wrong. The Nova car did not go very far in Latin-speaking countries because the name meant precisely that – 'no go'.

It is not always language that causes the problems. National Grid has to pay attention to different attitudes and cultural difference as regards communication preferences. For example, when seeking feedback over the telephone, US employees were very open and friendly, but were more likely to say what they thought the listener wanted to hear rather than express their true feelings. Conversely, UK employees tended to be more distant, suspicious and sceptical. Finding out exactly what works in terms of communication vehicle and activity can therefore be particularly challenging and less than straightforward.

There is a need to return to basics even when dealing with near neighbours in Europe and to understand that there is a fundamental difference between European and British approaches to employee communication.

Britain likes to take control of delivering the message, while the European approach is to negotiate and consult more. The clock is ticking on the requirement to adopt the more Continental line.

Even further afield, how you do not communicate rather than how you actually communicate can also play against you. A chief executive who failed to pay attention to the social niceties when visiting a Far Eastern division made the staff doubt the company's future. A mass exodus of staff was followed by a similar collapse in profit and the operation closed, largely due to a failure to spend some time on the seemingly pointless social round.

Mining company Rio Tinto is dispersed around the globe – over 260 locations in 40 countries from Australia to Kazakhstan and Mexico – and has 36,000 employees speaking a dozen or so languages. Often there may be only a handful of people in any one location but their communication needs are the same nonetheless. Each of its businesses has its own identity and is responsible for producing its own communications. However, communications from the centre go to a certain level of management who are responsible for cascading it.

Communications Advisor Mike Moser states: 'We recognise that there is always a need to adapt communication from the centre to the local market and we are proud of the diversity of our individual businesses' identities. The key phrase is to achieve consistency in our diversity.' An intranet-based website now enables all global communicators to post their latest news, corporate events, awards and communication products such as photography, company brochures and articles so they can be shared with group colleagues who may wish to learn from them.

Some aspects may not always be company specific. In South East Asia face-to-face communication may be more difficult to make work in the same ways as in the West due to traditional hierarchies that inhibit junior members of staff from questioning more senior staff.

However, community relations can play well as a motivator of employees as well as the local population itself. As in the UK, programmes which provide something extra, equipment for schools perhaps, can be well received.

Time differences are also something to take into particular account especially when attempting to set up video or audio conferencing. There are also cultural preferences: apparently voice mail is more popular in the United States than it is in the UK where there is a preference for group communication.

A technical point to consider when translating material is that some languages are particularly greedy for space. German articles are always much longer than the English equivalent. When translating from English a distillation of the key points may be sufficient.

The box below sets out a few overarching factors to take into account when considering global communication.

KEY FACTORS FOR INTERNATIONAL INTERNAL COMMUNICATION

- Time zones – not everyone is awake.
- Language – which one or ones?
- Cultural practice (how they do it).
- Social mores – class, gender, hierarchies.
- Listen to local people.
- Let the local people do the talking themselves.
- Use the appropriate spell checker – US for American English.
- Use nationals in country to translate.
- Just because English is spoken does not mean communication is understood.

Pamela Mounter has many years experience as an internal communicator with international reach. She has a wide variety of useful tips for the fledgling international internal communicator:

- Courtesy is all-important.
- Tone is also vital.
- Humour does not travel well.
- Slow down a little if English is not the first language.
- Pause and recap fairly frequently when giving a presentation or a speech.
- Simplify what you have to say and reduce the number of messages and topics.
- Restate any important statements stressing the word 'not' more than once (people mentally edit this out).

- Coach senior managers going overseas to give speeches in simple pleasantries in the language of the country. Even if they then resort back to English for the main part of their talk it at least shows they have been prepared to make an effort.
- Share best practice across locations.

Pamela Mounter once axed a global house magazine and replaced it with a news service which people in other countries could use as they saw fit. Head office apparently had some misgivings as they thought their messages would not get through. She argued that these messages would in fact have a better chance because they appeared in familiar local publications and people wanted to read the material as it included local information too. Sometimes the centrally produced material was condensed, but the whole exercise gave the local communicators an effective sense of ownership.

Training is another excellent way to gain trust. An editor in Azerbaijan was sent for training in the UK and the end result was a good-quality, well-respected local product. An added bonus was the addition to the central mix of communications of a fresh and interesting perspective.

Language is especially tricky. Pamela Mounter has a golden rule that everything must be translated by someone currently living in the country where it will be read. Even nationals now living abroad will lose some current nuances.

It is essential to ask people native to the country what works for them, even down to whether or not to keep a jacket on or off. Gestures can let you down and hand gestures are far from universal in their meaning.

When it comes to dress, women need to check whether it is OK to wear a sleeveless number, whether the length of their skirt or dress is right and if trousers are considered appropriate. In today's more sensitive climate it may be pertinent to ask when or if they should cover their hair in certain societies and under what circumstances.

'Dress down Fridays' where employees are allowed to dress more casually are not always appreciated. Some countries are very formal in their approach and this essentially American predilection can cause great angst.

Hierarchy is also important. You cannot simply go straight to whoever it is you wish to consult. You may need first to get agreement to the approach at the right levels. Those levels may transpire to be very different from what you would suppose to be appropriate.

One manager in Thailand adopted a creative and thoughtful approach when he wanted to secure a cross-section of views. This particular country is very hierarchical; you cannot leapfrog over corporate strata. He decided to run monthly birthday lunches open to anyone who had had a birthday in the preceding month, and this meant it was quite legitimate for all levels to be present. Even more importantly, no one took exception, seeing it as fun. The barriers came down and communication that would in the past have never taken place due to strict status rules was facilitated.

THE CONSULTANCY APPROACH

Globally dispersed communications consultancies must tackle these issues both for themselves and on behalf of their clients. Hill & Knowlton adopts a global but local approach on its own behalf to meet the needs of 2,000 employees in 70 offices spread across 34 countries.

Lindsay Eynon, Director of Change and Internal Communications, based in London, says her team works mainly in Europe, the Middle East and Africa (EMEA). The company language is English, as it is for many clients, but the local language, knowledge and cultural empathy is encouraged in many situations, to help bring the best of the mix to clients and Hill & Knowlton colleagues alike.

A key principle is to align external and internal communication and activity so that there is a seamless approach. What is being done on the outside of an organization should also ring true on the inside. This consistency helps to build trust between employees and the employer, and works both to protect and to enhance a company's external brand and reputation.

Most of the consultancy's internal communications work comes from clients helping people communicate change. Whatever function the client holds, this work usually includes close liaison with human resources and corporate communications teams, senior management and their in-house change project teams.

Sometimes clients use internal communication support as a stand-alone service, while in other circumstances such as significant restructuring, clients ask for an integrated range of internal and external communication services. So a critical skill for the Hill & Knowlton team is to be a 'chameleon', blending and shaping to fit the client's specific situation.

Hill & Knowlton is itself a large organization and knows only too well the challenges of internal communication across a diverse set of employees, countries, nationalities and specialities. From experience, it seems essential to learn to recognize and understand these differences and to find ways to benefit from them. Look for the core values that bind people together, and 'help people feel part of the team', no matter who or where you are.

THINGS TO THINK ABOUT – PAN-EMEA AND BEYOND

The professional communicator needs to weigh up not just where the message giver is coming from, but also the audience.

Social context can dictate how the most everyday and basic of communication is conducted. In some countries it is possible to send an e-mail request to an unknown individual and get a response as in Germany. However, in the Latin countries like Italy and Spain it is necessary to be formally introduced first.

In Asia Pacific asking personal questions about hobbies could well be seen as intrusive and irrelevant rather than an attempt to show an interest in an individual.

National cultures operate on a number of dimensions, one of which is power. In some cultures power is a given. In the United States an individual is accorded power if they have demonstrated they have achieved it. In Arab states power is given to the family, so it is inherited and is a given.

Change communications programmes originating in the United States will invariably be upbeat in tone. People in the UK, Germany and Holland do not respond quite so enthusiastically to this approach and prefer a more balanced approach, telling it as it is without the razzmatazz.

Communications style is explicit in the United States and the UK but implicit in Japan – where a lot of information and exchanges are hidden.

Decision making in Sweden is more consensus driven; you have to take time, but this gains ownership and engagement. In the United States, however, you might need to get everything signed in triplicate to make sure you actually have approval.

The theoretical approach is all very well, but practicalities can undermine the best-laid plans. Working hours may be different, bank holidays and religious festivals must not be overlooked – you can destroy your organization's credibility if you ignore these factors.

If you are working with Muslim countries you must allow for the practice of prayers; if you do not you will have broken the relationship.

It is important to use the appropriate media. In Saudi Arabia it is critical that it is face to face. The telephone is rated seventh in their priority list.

In some national and corporate cultures you have to arrange a meeting in advance, and in others you can simply stick your head around the door. A bureaucratic or personality-focused culture will determine which one works.

Different cultures will rate family, work and religion in differing orders of priority.

The canny international internal communicator must keep an eye on both the bigger structural picture formed by legal change and the smaller local picures affected by both country and corporate cultures.

As Wilson, Thomas-Derrick and Wright (2001) assert in *Strategic Communication Management*, no one size fits all. When operating in the global environment it is necessary to take account of language, culture and politics. To help your travelling manager adapt, provide an online global travel tool kit including handy material on local customs, business etiquette and cultural dos and don'ts.

KEY POINTS TO REMEMBER

- Native speakers living in the country concerned are the best translators/interpreters.
- Translate American English into British English and vice versa.
- Pay attention to differing attitudes and approaches applied on the ground.
- Not communicating is not an option.
- Allow space for written/spoken communication in languages like German – they take up more space.
- Enable local communicators to put their own stamp on centrally generated material.
- Head Office dress codes and habits do not always travel well.

Part 2

Getting it Right –
Practical Application

13

How to do it – setting about communication

Much early effort at internal communication may have gone adrift because it was carried out with little reference to the values of the organization. There is always so much to be done that it is tempting to dive straight in and get on with the task in hand. But without first establishing the key values of the organization you will be simply reacting and responding to circumstances rather than shaping them.

Taking the temperature of the organization may be no more complex than building up regular contact points at key parts of the organization with those individuals tasked to act as your eyes and ears, so that you in turn can provide a similar full-bodied view to your senior management.

Read your trade and specialist media to see how your organization is perceived in the way it performs and the way in which it treats employees and customers. This should give you a sound benchmark with which to compare the internal wishes and beliefs. It is unlikely you will find a complete match.

Make sure the internal communications function has a physical presence at any away-days the board or senior management may have planned in order to cast the runes and hopefully do rather more than navel gaze. This all sounds great, except of course if you work in one of the many organizations which does not automatically grant you equal status or access to the boardroom. How do you get on board?

Through your elementary research you should have established the key matters of concern. Be prepared to support your argument even if it does not appear to be espousing the current values. You need to establish where there is disparity between what the board thinks is happening and the real blockages on the ground, and suggest how to bridge them. Identifying the territory in between the reality and the corporate goal and placing a substantiated value on it should provide the tools to get you noticed. The bottom line and whatever is stopping the organization from achieving the ideal position is what most grabs the attention and imagination of the board. Learn to read and interpret a balance sheet (this is not a subject for this book and there are very many other books and courses to help you).

Like corporate communication, the internal communications function has the perfect excuse to stick its nose in everywhere. Do not just demonstrate your value to the top – practise those skills on other departments like human resources, finance, production, distribution and marketing. As with all relationships there is nothing more attractive than an apparently interested audience. Being a good listener may be one of the most important and valuable skills you can develop.

Determining whether or not the organization has the right core values and determining precisely what these should be are not your job per se, but you can act as a barometer and reflect back the reality from both without and within the organization.

This should be done as part of your routine practice. The communication process and its vital components are shown in Figure 13.1.

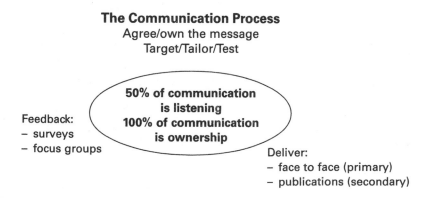

Figure 13.1 *The communication process – basic components to be built in*

WHAT YOUR PEOPLE WANT TO HEAR

It is sometimes hard to get away from the 'us and them' clichés of the old school industrial management.

Center and Jackson (1995) carried out a study for the International Association of Business Communicators and came up with the following (see panel below).

SUBJECTS OF INTEREST TO EMPLOYEES

Rank	Subject	Scale 1–10
1	Organizational plans for the future	8
2	Job advancement opportunities	7
3	Job related how-to information	7
4	Productivity improvements	6
5	Personnel policies and practices	6
6	How we're doing vs the competition	6
7	How my job fits into the organization	6
8	How external events affect job	5
9	How profits are used	5
10	Financial results	4

This provides a pretty good checklist for the preparation of any short or long term communication programmes. Your job is to find material from within the organization that fits into these categories.

Arnott (1986) puts all this rather more prosaically when he quotes Roger d'Aprix, former Head of Internal Communications at Xerox, who reframed staff needs along Maslow's hierarchy of needs model. He reckons workers require answers to the 'I' questions before they move on to the 'we' questions.

The 'I' questions ask:

- What's my job?
- How am I doing?
- Does anybody give a damn?

Once answers to the above are satisfactorily given and processed, the questions asked are:

- How are we doing?
- How do we fit in to the whole?
- How can I help?

Your role as communicator is to balance the above against the requirements of management and be prepared for some stiff debate where the two might diverge. Be prepared to upset one or even both sides of the equation rather more frequently than you would suppose or might like. Diplomacy and tact are crucial characteristics you will need to develop, plus a nose for finding alternative sources of information.

The newcomer to internal communication needs to establish the extent of the resources available to them. It is unlikely you will have your own printing press to hand; you may have to focus the department digital camera and wield a mean pen. Only you know your key strengths and it is best to be honest with yourself and play to them.

Increasingly external media are complaining that the young PROs they are encountering do not know what the media wants and are unable to write in an easy to read and digestible manner.

A special plea: writing dissertations for a degree are not the same as writing short, snappy and deathless prose for a newspaper. A glance at the average tabloid national newspaper will show you that. Perhaps your skills lie more strategically in the thinking and planning rather than the execution and delivery. The following chapters look at the nuts and bolts of delivering key communication activities.

But the most important aspect for you to focus on is being clear as to why you are saying something, to whom you are saying it, how you are going to transmit it and then measuring your results.

Russell Grossman, Head of Internal Communication, BBC, has a neat way of marshalling types of communication which are conducted on a daily or less frequent basis. The basic purpose is 'Talking the right language, creating passion, understanding and commitment'. The structure is outlined in the panel opposite.

To round off this chapter, a case study from north of the border. Internal communications was formalized only recently for VisitScotland, formerly the Scottish Tourist Board, a 'non-departmental public body' funded by the Scottish Executive. Here is how they went about it.

VisitScotland builds internal capacity

Based in Edinburgh, VisitScotland has offices in London and Inverness and employs 193 people, 64 of whom are field-based quality assurance advisers. Much of its experience of the internal communication function in the past had been patchy if not non-existent. A management review underlined the need to communicate developmental and organizational milestones in a more formalized way.

VisitScotland was also about to undergo radical change with a new structure and senior management team; communicating this in a more measured way was regarded as vital for the success of restructuring.

INTERNAL COMMUNICATION SPECTRUM

Day to Day Communication

- organization news;
- awards, etc;
- housekeeping – pay, appraisals, appointments, operational, etc;
- interpreting external media coverage;
- listening and responding to worries, etc.

Change Communication

- explaining vision, purpose and values;
- helping leaders talk with their teams;
- sharing knowledge and best practice;
- embedding change initiatives;
- listening for reactions;
- understanding responses to change;
- celebrating team success;
- industry and other 'bigger picture' news.

Marketing Communication

- creating passion about product;
- internal marketing activity;
- inviting critique and discussion;
- marketing programmes;
- visual environment (buildings etc).

External crises also hit in the form of foot and mouth disease and the World Trade Center attack which, combined with a global downturn, brought the organization into the public spotlight and not always in a flattering light.

A survey conducted with the employees underlined the need for clearer internal communication supported by the directors and board, a more formal communication of the future role of the organization, opportunity for employee empowerment and scope to gain greater understanding of the roles of colleagues.

To get the ball rolling a group of employees from various departments was set up to concentrate on the project. Their objectives were to communicate and champion the values of VisitScotland, launch a new way of communicating internally, build confidence in the organization and get support for the culture changes. They also aimed to create a seamless organization in which everyone was working together, wanted to raise morale and keep employees involved in and informed about the change process.

A series of initiatives was identified for swift action – implementing a staff survey, conducting a communications audit and setting up a dedicated internal communications team. Other initiatives included opportunities to meet with the management team, staff awareness sessions, monthly newsletter, major event and new intranet. So successful was the effort that a new communication group was proposed to keep up support and feedback for the new initiatives.

Employees saw the first stage of the intranet introduced in May 2002, providing news and information; its second phase was implemented in spring 2003.

Meetings with the new chief executive and directors were well received. Also helpful were the staff awareness sessions run simultaneously at all three sites on the one day. There were also presentations from different groups and departments which served to update progress towards the new organizational structure and culture.

An electronic monthly newsletter, *Outlook*, was sent out over a period of 10 months. This included people news, corporate updates and facts, had live links and a feedback facility.

An employee opinion survey conducted in December 2002 looked at the organization's performance against similar bodies undergoing similar change and early results showed it had performed well.

The new intranet that replaced an earlier version contained a staff directory with photographs and job descriptions, a news section on business developments and other industry news. Also included were new ideas, corporate plans, projects from each department, financial and human resources procedures, briefings and factsheets and corporate presentations. Maps, organizational charts, links, social news including a chatroom, corporate database and photo library, competitions, new employee induction pack and a room-booking service were also added. To keep the 'hub' well stocked, 'news heralds' were appointed from the workforce.

To show how far everyone had come, a hard-copy publication in the form of a review of the year *ReVisitScotland* was published. A dedicated internal communication team comprising a knowledge manager, internal communications officer and intranet coordinator has been set up and located in the communication department, although it works closely with human resources. The organization looks set fair for whatever the future throws at it.

KEY POINTS TO REMEMBER

- Do not take for granted the health of your organization – take regular soundings to check.
- See how outsiders view the organization.
- Develop your listening skills.
- Employees most want to know about future plans and how they fit in.
- Be honest about your own abilities to deliver.
- Establish what skills you need to buy in.

14

We can all talk can't we? Face to face

Many surveys conducted into employees' preferred mode of communication suggest that the all-time favourite remains face to face. This chapter will focus on logistical aspects of improving the conditions for dialogue in one-to-one or group situations.

Communication coach Johnny Harben believes the internal communicator now has the golden opportunity to lead on all levels of communication, starting with the rediscovery of narrative and ending with the killing off of PowerPoint-style presentations. To demonstrate his points on the former he outlines how easyJet absorbed rival airline Go.

LISTENING IN ON EASY CONVERSATION

'An organization in conversation with itself': this was the stated, overall purpose of easyJet's internal communication activity when in 2002 Bridgeen Rea took responsibility for the IC role. The low-cost airline had just announced the takeover of Go.

She put the emphasis on conversations – essentially unrehearsed dialogue – in easyJet. Her job was to feed this grapevine with attractive, accurate and trustworthy news and information on the one hand. On the other, she was to listen to feedback by providing opportunities for people to be in regular conversations with leaders and managers in order to discuss and challenge what was going on around the workplace. Her daily work was about the intrinsic (how people talk to each other) rather than the instrumental.

Experts say that what is relevant to face-to-face conversation applies just as much to telephone communication, the biggest traffic in most organizations. The telling of stories or narratives is a major component and is central to conversational success.

Even the simplest of events is dramatised in 'coffee machine' stories, often with no great skill ('I was at my desk, right? And the phone goes. And guess who it is? It's Jenny and she's all over the place. She says to me (mimics) "I've just handed my notice in", well?')

Story telling is central to being human, and stories or narratives – the terms are interchangeable – cross all history and arise in all circumstances. Stories in this sense are not fables, lies or fairy tales. They are the way humans understand, experience, communicate and try to influence others. Stories constantly change as people pass them on and consist of the process of telling as well as the end product. Corporate culture may therefore be regarded as a set of connecting stories.

This is a style that is engaging and embracing, aspirationally open and honest. In considering your organization's style it might be wise to adopt some principles for effective conversation. This may be published in the form of a communication agreement or contract.

The 'Communication Contract':

1. Everyone is entitled to receive daily news of what is going on around the whole business by any reasonable means. In return, everyone agrees to see this news as often as possible and to respond and contribute as they wish, including questioning and challenging.
2. Everyone is entitled to a regular one-to-one meeting with his or her manager. In return everyone agrees to be as honest and open in these meetings as possible so as to make them effective for all parties.
3. Everyone is entitled to access to the intranet. In return, everyone agrees to use this resource as often as possible and to respond and contribute as they wish, including questioning and challenging.
4. Everyone is entitled to a regular meeting of their natural work-team, at least once a month, with their manager present, when they can discuss and challenge what is going on for their team and for the organization as a whole. In return everyone is expected to contribute to these meetings by following some simple rules for effective dialogue.

In addition, communicators may need to provide a course in the essentials of good dialogue, including best practice in meetings. In the field of communication it is increasingly recognized that the emphasis in terms of personal development needs to be placed on a manager's competence in face-to-face dialogue more than on the use of formal media such as e-mail, memos and such aids as PowerPoint. Audio-visual aids such as PowerPoint enable presenters to get caught up in the mechanics of the technology at the expense of the core messages and values.

Communicators should be helping leaders and managers by getting them to ask themselves three questions before they start to frame a presentation for more than eight or ten staff or a team conversation: 'What do I want people to understand, feel, do as a result of this input?'

The question will often lead to the use of stories or narratives, for example stories about the best of what is happening in the organization already, or things that could be done more extensively in the service of a new strategy.

It becomes obvious that it is easier to get people thinking and feeling differently about something if both their hearts and their minds are engaged. Their minds might have turned off if the story of the new strategy implied that everything that had gone before had been rubbish, because it can be seen as criticism of their own prior efforts.

Johnny Harben's conclusions: learn more about conversation and dialogue, talk to colleagues about the benefits of a 'communication agreement' and banish PowerPoint.

HOW OTHERS DO IT

Demonstrating a greater propensity for the other side of dialogue – effective listening – is critical. Buckinghamshire County Council has put in place the necessary mechanisms for this by developing a system of elected employee representatives from each of its services as part of increasing employee engagement and involvement in decision making. Quite separate from recognized union representation, they work on major projects. This supplements a wide range of communications activities including a newsletter, intranet and video.

In managing even the smallest of meetings there are ways of getting the most from coming together by at least establishing the right conditions for the whole activity to be both comfortable for the participants and effective for the organization. The box below sets out some aspects to consider.

KEY POINTS TO GETTING THE MOST FROM YOUR MEETING

- Draw up an agenda.
- Send it out in good time.
- Lay on something nice to eat – chocolate cake, biscuits.
- Be generous with the tea, coffee and bottled water.
- Keep to the agenda.
- Get everyone to contribute.
- Make sure the meeting is minuted.
- Finish on time.
- Ensure minutes go out quickly.

Some organizations feel you can get too comfortable and have introduced meetings with no chairs. In these days of litigation and the Disability Discrimination Act this would not be wise, especially if you are aware that some of your staff have physical difficulties. This kind of approach also suggests a lack of courtesy at the very least. There are ways to make a room comfortable without reducing the effectiveness of the meeting and a firm, clear agenda managed by an equally firm, focused chairperson will ensure the meeting achieves its set goals.

Keep the room well ventilated but not too chilly and this will ensure everyone stays awake. If you are planning to meet in that well-known 'graveyard' slot after lunch, pick a controversial or energetic speaker or a challenging or important subject to kick off with – that way no one will want to nod off.

Entertainment seems to be an underlying theme of this section and as Johnny Harben said, one of the biggest killers can be misuse of presentation aids. But it is not just PowerPoint and other computerized systems that are to blame – overhead projectors, flipcharts and even old-fashioned slide shows can be just as deadening to the imagination of the presenter and by extension the audience.

However, one of the most engaging presentations the author ever witnessed was on a dreary November evening in a badly lit cellar wine bar. The speaker had no aids other than two flipcharts he had dragged across London by bus. He placed them either side of him and spent the evening diving between the two which had been ready prepared with his key points. Five years on it is still possible to remember the underlying message about homelessness charity, Crisis.

OVERCOMING PRESENTATION SICKNESS

The best lessons are not always the new ones. Below are some key pointers on giving presentations.

KEY POINTS FOR PRESENTATION AIDS

- Use a large typeface.
- No more than seven words across.
- No more than seven lines down.
- Turn projector off when talking and not presenting.
- Talk about contents and not something else.
- Skip the distracting graphics.
- Avoid lots of tints, or try colours out in advance.
- Provide legible handouts.

It is something of a judgement call whether you give out handouts before or after a presentation. Before, and you may risk the participants being distracted by them. Provide pads of paper and pens for those congenitally unable to bring their own – a surprisingly large number.

But why stick to the same old format? Howard Krais at law firm Eversheds has perfected the art of the roadshow for a notoriously hard-to-engage audience.

Popcorn seems to be a magic ingredient. Taking cinema as the theme, staff called to the roadshow were invited to 'have your say at the movies', which expanded on earlier 'have your say' quarterly sessions held in each of the regional centres.

Just as in the real movies, 'advertisements' were used to ensure the audience knew what to expect. To accompany the 'films' or videos, popcorn was served. Fun appears to be a crucial but often overlooked element, but a lot of hard work is also needed to make sure the mechanics work.

The practical elements that should be taken into account are listed in the following panel.

LOGISTICS OF MANAGING A ROADSHOW

- Establish objectives of event.
- Ensure these match with other activities.
- Make sufficient rooms available.
- Check that rooms are large enough for main groups.
- And small enough for discussion groups.
- Brief presenters thoroughly.
- Prepare scripts for presenters.
- Shift pace by interspersing video with live 'acts'.
- Provide the right balance of presenters (board, senior manager, functional heads).
- Ensure presenters have rehearsed sufficiently.
- Make sure presenters are happy to improvise.
- Provide back-up if presenter drops dead en route.
- Anticipate problems with transport for speaker or audience.

Every exchange in the workplace between two people or more is an opportunity for dialogue. The way ahead is to make these exchanges work effectively alongside more formal channels of communication.

KEY POINTS TO REMEMBER

- Hang out by the water cooler if you want to know what people think.
- Stories are how people share information – use the format.
- Set some ground rules for effective corporate conversations.
- Emphasize everyone's responsibility to communicate.
- Be clear why a meeting is happening and communicate that.
- Take care of participants – feed and water them.
- Do not use technology as a conversational crutch.

15

The creative aspects – writing, editing and designing it yourself

Ever spotted a strange little figure in an unexpected location scribbling furiously? Do not assume they are unwell; they could have been grabbed by the muse and are busy capturing their inspiration before it is gone again.

Probably the most difficult thing to teach anyone is creativity. It always seems that if you cannot draw a straight line, fashion design and the like are barred in terms of career. And if you did not win an essay competition in childhood you probably feel you cannot write for a living. You may wonder what place creativity has in the grand scheme that is internal communications. In Chapter 13 the list of subjects the workforce wanted to be kept in the know about did not exactly reek of the most imaginative things.

But without that inspired spark most of what passes for consumer advertising would be reduced to mere exhortations on newness and cost. It is often that something extra that sells the brand and this is unlikely to come from a straightforward translation of the balance sheet.

There is no intention in this chapter to teach you how to write or to take award winning or even serviceable photographs. Instead, using some examples presented by research for this book and a few tricks of the trade learnt from years at the journalistic coalface, the author hopes you will be more confident in your own creative ability or able at the very least to intelligently brief specialists (see Chapter 21 for more on this).

CAPTURING THE SPARK

Getting started on a written piece is always the hardest part, but once the first two or three paragraphs are written the rest just seem to flow naturally. The point of the story of the huddled figure is that inspiration can and is more likely to strike away from the constantly ringing telephones and other interruptions of everyday working life.

Much has been said about individuals (some creative geniuses and others not recognized as such) going to sleep on a difficult problem and dreaming or at least waking up with the solution. And these solutions are not always bizarre nonsensical duds – some work.

Both the act of going on a long walk or waking up shouting 'Eureka!' may work simply because the mind has been let off the leash and can roam more freely.

So where and when do you get your best ideas? Is it in the shower at the end of the day? Is it just before you go to sleep or when you wake up? Is it at work – on your own with the voice mail taking calls, or in a group in a set-piece situation?

It may make for messy living, but why not dot your most likely thinking spots with a small pad of paper and pencil (in the bathroom) or, for less damp surroundings, pen. It is also possible to buy pocket-sized notebooks to capture your thoughts on the move. Perhaps you would prefer a more technologically driven approach. A mini cassette player would work well in the car and will also fit neatly into a handbag.

SPARKING IDEAS TOGETHER

Different pieces of research have from time to time suggested that an individual might produce more ideas on their own than the combined efforts of a group working together. This has also been applied to e-mail fora with conflicting results.

Nick Fitzherbert from Magic Management speaking at the Chartered Institute of Public Relations National Conference in November 2003 declared travelling as the best opportunity for idea generation at 39 per cent. Apparently only 11 per cent found inspiration while at work and only 1 per cent more found it in the shower, while 18 per cent preferred sleeping on it.

Despite work's poor showing he has some tips for effective brainstorming as illustrated in the boxed panel below.

THE IDEAL BRAINSTORM

- Six individuals with different skills (experts, novices, chair, recorder).
- Equipment to record.
- No alcohol.
- Not too much comfort.
- Strict timeframe.
- Clear objectives.
- Broad ownership and status of ideas.
- All ideas encouraged, none dismissed.

It may seem odd to place such a firm structure around what is supposed to be creative activity, but it is the only way to ensure that goals are achieved.

Out of all the ideas generated probably 90 per cent will be jettisoned. It is therefore important that no one is criticized for having supposedly wild, impractical ideas. Everyone entering into the process should be completely happy with the notion that few ideas will actually get on let alone off the drawing board and that no shame or blame is implied.

Peter Lawlor, Creative Director at Hill & Knowlton consultancy, reckons that when a child is five there are few barriers, and if a child chooses to draw a blue cow then such an entity is deemed possible. Children do not filter ideas so seemingly impossible ones are explored, and adults would do well to relearn that skill, at least in part.

Nick Fitzherbert describes four levels of brainstorming. Word association is a bit like sticking a pin in a thesaurus (incidentally a great way to find a name for something) and involves playing games with words associated with an object and then working with the resulting thoughts.

Free thinking is, exactly as the label suggests, an opportunity to range far and wide with a given subject, and several consultancies run creative thinking programmes for their clients.

Tested strategies, however, are the opposite, taking ideas that have already worked elsewhere and then giving them an extra twist. This one probably works where an extension of a ready-developed programme is needed.

Marginal or magical mindset is the search for different perspectives. Moving to an unusual location may work here and may involve bringing in people from outside the nominal group or perhaps sending individuals off to work alone. This approach might also lend itself to reversal of the usual circumstances – turning the problem on its head before seeking an answer.

Even the colours in the meeting room could have some bearing on the success or otherwise of the session. Nick Fitzherbert says red generates excitement, yellow lifts mood, blue calms, white can be sterile but also uncluttered, while green is peaceful. A bowl of nuts will also get the participants buzzing – apparently boosting serotonin levels – again all to do with mood.

Brainstorming is not restricted to strict idea generation. It can also be used as part of the communications process as demonstrated below.

SEXING UP THE MISSION STATEMENT

A solo brainstorm in advance of a team presentation resulted in the brainstorming technique itself being used to get staff at the Royal Bank of Scotland thinking about the bank's core values. A relatively long-serving team member had to give a presentation to a monthly team meeting and decided to emphasize the organization's mission statement by bringing it to life in an unexpected way. There were penalties for not knowing key elements, so she sought to find a memorable way of making it all stick. What better way than using that age-old motivator – sex.

She employed one of Nick Fitzherbert's techniques – word association. So the phrase 'fit for purpose' became 'condom', 'interdependence' became '69', 'individual responsibility' – 'birth control'. The group were asked to supply the rest, which they did with great humour.

Humour was also crucial to BSkyB's attempts to get a largely youthful workforce thinking about a sharesave programme. Speaking at the CIPR's November 2003 conference, Group Head of Internal Communications, Hamish Haynes, employed bags of chocolate coins to get the message across entertainingly.

THINK VISUALLY

Many of the best ideas are in fact visual and summon up ready-made images. There has been a tendency in recent years to use little better than passport-sized photographs to illustrate articles. In an otherwise expensive or good-looking publication this could project meanness, perhaps an unfortunate subliminal message. There is an old adage that a picture is worth a thousand words – you can test the veracity of that by having a look at any national or regional newspaper. These publications also give space generously to pictures that warrant the treatment; do the same.

And it is the idea that counts. A long line-up around a cheque presentation, or a group shot of an entire team may suit an economically driven photographic unit (local papers sell more prints of team photos) but it does not progress the story. A good photograph should emphasize or illustrate a point. Careful positioning on the page will often draw the eye in. Use an eye-catching image on the front page to entice people to look on the inside by teasing them with a few relevant details.

Whether you are briefing a photographer or taking the image yourself, bear certain things in mind. Make sure your subject is comfortable with what you have in mind, including the final usage of the image. They may have an added twist of their own which would give a better result. Be careful of timing for photo shoots – avoid mid- to late afternoon as from autumn through to early summer the available light will surely let you down. Photographs are probably best taken in the morning unless night is part of the context.

If you cannot afford to brief a photographer or take your own images, an option is presented by any one of the many photo libraries now in existence. Catalogues of literally thousands of images can be accessed online. Just remember you are buying on a one-off use basis only, unless you have negotiated otherwise. It is also possible that your chosen image will be used elsewhere.

You may also wish to consider whether colour or black and white strikes the right chord for your audience. Black and white does not always have to appear old-fashioned; it can effectively generate atmosphere compared with the same image in colour.

And if you do have to use a poor picture because it is the only one available, do what the national papers do: use it big.

Of course photographs are just one kind of visual element. Sketches and drawings can be appropriate and often make a point more subtly than the gritty realism of a photograph. It is most likely that such images would need to be commissioned and there is a graphic designer out there with the right touch for you.

Digital cameras allow the insertion of still or moving images into websites so there is no reason why the intranet should be regarded as a purely static medium. Overall tips on intranet and technologically driven platforms are covered in Chapter 19.

BACK TO THE WRITTEN WORD

If a picture is worth a thousand words you will still need words for the caption. Pictures alone cannot provide the necessary context. So this chapter culminates with tips on writing for publications which apply equally internally and externally.

There are tips worth learning from the mass media about the way words are employed on the page. Dissertation-style writing is no use for an internal newspaper. First, it is necessary to establish what your readers would usually choose to read in terms of national newspapers and as far as is practical mimic the style.

Once upon a time there was a rule that there should be a maximum of 40 words for an 'intro' (introductory paragraph) and 30 for subsequent paragraphs. Nowadays it is likely to be shorter still, especially for publications with an external audience. These rules are made to be broken – have a look at the occasional headline in the *Guardian* which reads like a fully fledged sentence or paragraph. However, use this particular technique sparingly.

People are interested in other people, especially ones they know or who are like themselves. Finding a human aspect to a corporate story will ensure it has a better chance of being read and its key points understood.

How to go about adding a bit of humanity to your copy? You might go in search of the hero who kept the machines running against all the odds, the champion runner who excels both in and outside work, a winner of an industry prize. Interviews provide the opportunity to put key points in someone else's words.

You should also try to make your copy as active as possible. Always use a simple word rather than the jargon or complex version – 'mother' is so much better than 'maternal parent'.

Why not use your organization's own employees to conduct interviews with the top brass? The genuine voice will then come through. The LE Group's *Livewire* publication makes a regular feature of such interviews. Careful editing appears to help retain much of the flavour of the original writer's voice.

MANAGING THE EDITORIAL PANEL

Many publications boast extensive editorial committees and these can often be the death of a lively publication unless the expert – you – manages them.

If at all possible try to whittle down to the barest minimum the number of people who can reject copy. With any luck, if you demonstrate you will not abuse their trust, the approval process will become little more than a formality.

Meetings can be restricted to one at the planning stage, which can also serve to review the previous issue, and another at the basic copy-checking stage. Positioning stories should be left to your discretion except to take account of the corporate weighting of particular issues.

If the panel is large why not use this to your advantage by making each individual responsible for generating and collecting ideas from their specific work area? This makes them feel far more involved in the whole process.

IT'S THE OVERALL LOOK THAT COUNTS

Along with photography, images and words, there is one last aspect – the overall look of the publication. Depending on the format you have chosen, or have to work with, why not steal a leaf out of your commercial counterpart's book? Even a newsletter can look much more newsy if a scaled-down approach to newspaper design is adopted. Headlines should be more than just labels – make them active and use as few words as possible. Do, however, make sure that your chosen gems in combination mean what you want them to say – it is possible to be too economical at times.

Look at facing pages together rather than separately. Where possible avoid whole banks of headlines running across the top of one, let alone both, pages. Photographs, drawings, logos and bylines (a chance to give credit where it is due) help to break up such runs. Cross-heads or boxes containing quotes from the copy can be used to build in natural breaks to vast slabs of copy.

When choosing photographs remember to place a face so that it faces into rather than out of the page. If you do not do this the reader's eye will travel off the page and they could be lost to you forever. However, you can break this rule on the front page as a means of encouraging people to follow up a story within. Catchy captions help the process.

There are also arguments about whether people read from the front or the back of a publication. There is no one correct answer but good signposting in the form of contents panels will ensure they get to where they want to go. If sport has always resided on the back page you tinker with this tradition at your peril, particularly as it is something of a mass media tradition.

WHAT TO PUT IN

Bear in mind the wise words of the author's first boss in journalism: 'What is written with interest is read with interest'. If you cannot make the effort to inject your own interest into a subject, why should your readers bother?

HOW TO MAKE YOUR PUBLICATION GRAB ATTENTION

- Get a professional redesign that you can follow (template).
- Pick a title you can live with.*
- Take tips on writing from your favourite newspaper.
- Go for snappy headlines.
- Pull out quotes to break up copy.
- Use cross-heads to assist the eye.
- Use professionally produced photography.
- Brief the photographer but let the professional do their job.
- Place the pictures to catch the eye.
- Do not run headlines across in banks of twos and threes.

It is worth testing the name of any publication with parts of the readership you can trust for an honest answer. Your brainstormed gem could well have a meaning you never anticipated. Should the magazine be despatched overseas it is well worth getting the local dictionary out too.

Stuck for content generally? Well, go back to Chapter 13 and use Center and Jackson's (1995) checklist to establish what your audience wants to know about. Give them the news of the organization, but also remember to add the human interest aspects too.

THE ANNUAL REPORT

For many organizations producing the annual report is a major headache, but here a creative approach can pay dividends. A health board used the Harry Potter school of publishing and produced different covers for different audiences, and presented the content in a blockbuster novel style.

Whatever you do, pick a form that excites. Charity Volunteer Reading Help which encourages children to read produced its report like the end-of-year reports so familiar to parents – all those ticks and crosses worked a treat. Content does, however, need to include a clear explanation of accounts and statements from on high. But there is also ample opportunity to share excellent practice from the different corners of the organization. Why not let the teams talk in their own words? The images will also enliven things too.

* A local authority which shall remain nameless launched an internal newsletter called *Corporation Tips* in the belief this was witty. Perhaps it was but workers, particularly those working at the 'tip' (the works depot) end of the business, were not amused and employee relations were put back years. The publication was short lived.

It is important to remember precisely who will be the audience for your annual report. If your organization is a charity it will have very many external audiences including the Charity Commission and potential donors. It may pay you to consider producing more than one version – one for the external audiences and one for the internal.

Although the accounts side of things will not be part of the internal communicator's role as a rule, you should ensure you understand precisely what the figures are saying so that your messages are consistent with the organization's true position. An upbeat tone may not work too well in times of stress. Whatever you write should also be cleared with the investor relations team to ensure consistency.

The annual report also offers the opportunity for the internal communicator to work more closely with the organization's public relations people. Harness them to uncover stories that might appeal internally and vice versa.

The next chapter touches on the logistics of publication production.

KEY POINTS TO REMEMBER

- Be prepared for the creative muse to strike in odd places – waterproof pad in the shower.
- Use journeys for thinking time.
- Brainstorms need structure and rules to work.
- Make use of a variety of techniques like word association to get groups buzzing.
- Before briefing a photographer visualize the image you want achieved.
- Use imagery on the printed page to encourage people to read on.
- Read both tabloid and broadsheet newspaper to gauge writing style.
- Keep paragraphs and sentences short and sweet.
- Find the human aspect to your story.
- Cut jargon.
- Get the workforce to interview the bosses.
- Keep your editorial board manageable and manage them.
- Go for a newsy overall appearance.

16

Publishing the printed word – the logistical aspects

There was a time in the mid- to late 1990s when it was firmly believed that the printed publication had had its day and we would all be reading our employee publications straight off our computer screens. It will be some time before the 'i-book' is perfected to overcome its inherent disadvantages. Only in a limited number of cases have all publications been moved online, and usually only in appropriate technology-based companies. Some organizations may have reduced the number of printed publications but they still exist alongside the e-version, ensuring employees without constant access to a terminal are kept in touch.

However, producing print can be expensive and it remains something of a numbers game. The first thousand copies of anything will carry a bulk share of the costs as it bears the cost of typesetting, artwork, platemaking and proofs plus other intermediate stages.

Quantities beyond the initial thousand will be rather cheaper as you are being charged for paper, ink and collation alone. However, should you miscalculate and return for reprints you will be charged the set-up costs all over again because plates are not always stored and some have a limited lifespan anyway. It pays to calculate print runs very carefully. Should storage prove an issue, talk sweetly to the printer who may have capacity and be able to assist.

USING THE PROFESSIONAL TYPESETTER AND PRINTER

You can save time and money to some extent by using desktop publishing packages which combine typesetting and layout functions, previously the province of inky old craftsmen. However, the finish you achieve is unlikely to be as impressive as that of a professional.

Copy can be transmitted electronically to a professional typesetter either by disk or e-mail but it is up to you to have checked it first. Failure to check copy is one of the single greatest causes of unexpected price hikes in the middle of print jobs. Author's proofs can add substantially to cost and also take time.

It is also possible for the occasional print professional to prove to be dyslexic. Even if the copy is your own deathless prose and left you in a pristine and accurate state, you still need to check each set of proofs in turn. Amazingly mistakes can creep in somewhere between you and the printer's version.

Should you be working on a directory or listing-style format, or a publication with headings, always check that these are where you want them placed on a page. Even changing one small word can cause everything else in the document to shift and throw out of alignment your carefully planned design elements. But the most important point is that constant copy changes will add to the bill and certainly will not improve your temper.

If you need to make corrections at proof stage, follow standard proof correction practice as shown in Foster (2001). His volume *Effective Writing Skills for Public Relations* provides much-needed guidance on a whole range of related issues relating to writing and publication style generally.

Make sure at contract stage that the price agreed makes allowance for reasonable author's corrections, and have a guide as to what is regarded as reasonable. Ensure you are not in fact going to be charged for putting right the printer's errors.

Paper probably constitutes one of the largest elements of cost in any printing project. Different weights of paper can have an enormous bearing on the budget generally, especially in those cost centres relating to postage. Before finalizing a contract with your commercial printer it is sensible to look at how different qualities and weights of paper work, not just in terms of physical weight but also how they carry the ink itself.

A large print run of a tabloid-style publication may seem appropriate on a newsprint weight. Even if you refrain from using too much high-density colour photography or tint panels you could still experience what is termed 'bleed-through'. Try reading a page of newsprint against daylight or strong light; if the paper is too low in weight or quality you will find words and pictures from following pages grinning through whatever you are reading. This can also prove true of qualities of paper other than newsprint.

It is possible to produce a newspaper-style publication on a glossy paper, but this is more than likely costlier than newsprint. This may, however, be an appropriate alternative depending on the nature of your audience and its expectations. High-gloss or shiny paper, depending on how copy and images are used in terms of scale, can also communicate subliminal messages both good or bad. In some cases glossy can translate as tacky and downmarket and so may best be reserved for magazine formats.

Heavier-weight matt paper is rather more versatile in that it can be used on all types of publication from newspapers through newsletters to magazines. The better-quality papers can also have a rather more pleasant feel than gloss, so again be swayed by your audience.

In certain public sector and not-for-profit arenas if economic conditions are hard using a heavy-weight paper where something lighter had sufficed previously could exude an unfortunate message of profligacy. However, choosing too thin a paper can transmit a very different message – that of lack of care or a warning of tough times to come.

DEPLOYING COLOUR AND TYPEFACE

Few publications appear on colour papers and it is not simply because they tend to cost more or their creators are old-fashioned. For most readers apart from those with sight problems the easiest combination to read is black print on white paper. Colour panels should be used sparingly, especially on newsprint weights of paper. Do not be tempted to use more than a 10 or 20 per cent wash of colour (or tint as it is more properly termed) even if you are planning to use a very heavy-weight typeface.

You can break this rule when using black or deep colours, setting the type in white. However, these are best restricted to very small boxes or panels perhaps for the author's byline, headlines or introductory panels.

Should you decide to use colour in this way, pay particular attention to the kind of typeface you plan to use. There are two basic types: sans serif or serif. Sans serif faces do not have the serifs or short lines at the end of the character. Sans serif faces such as Gill will be harder to read for any length of time and Times and other serif faces are easier on the eye. Serif faces may look somewhat old-fashioned but they still manage to do the job and get read effectively.

To achieve some degree of consistency in the look of printed material it is wise to restrict yourself in terms of the numbers of typefaces you choose. You may select one for headlines and another for body copy – two, perhaps three, different families of type but no more. You may use the different faces to flag up a change of pace – perhaps serif for news and sans serif for features or vice versa.

Within each typeface a range of different treatments is possible which can be used effectively for headlines, photograph captions and pull-out quotes. Upright versions of typefaces will be described as Roman whereas a script effect will be Italic. You can also use expanded or condensed versions of them all, bold or regular. But it is worth checking the effect before venturing in that direction. Again use them sparingly for greatest impact.

It may also be possible that some of your employees may have disabilities which render certain media inaccessible to them. Charities looking after the interests of people with physical disabilities can advise you. When producing print publications or, for that matter, online newsletters it is worth increasing the point size – that means even shorter stories! Cross-heads and the like help take the eye comfortably through the maze of print. Remember that your prized newspaper or e-mail publication is still likely to be a second, third or fourth choice with voice communication still the media of choice.

Back to colour aspects. Colour panels can be used to enliven a largely cheap black and white newsletter format. Mastheads carrying the publication name can look more eye catching as black or white out of a heavy tint. If you have to photocopy, or think there is any chance the recipients will, it is a good idea to see how certain colour combinations react. Black out of deep mauve or aubergine will translate as black with no definition. Pale yellow often disappears as an effect altogether.

Colours on glossy or matt publications can hide some unexpectedly nasty and embarrassing surprises. A souvenir guide for a hospital which used the corporate blue (a particularly deep shade and a fairly standard colour) on the cover transferred itself to the royal white gloves. In fact the blue redistributed itself for many years to come. Make sure your printer either provides a protective coating to seal the colour (another extra cost), consider a different paper, or ensure it is properly dried.

PAGINATION AND OTHER WEIGHTY ISSUES

Page counts are an important consideration, particularly on the cost front. Depending on the type of publication you are producing you may wish to look at printing copy on inside covers to make use of otherwise redundant space. Each page of print you produce usually comes as one of four – so you usually talk about a 4-, 8-, 12- page etc publication. If you can only fill three you do not get a reduction for space unfilled.

Using full colour throughout a publication can prove to be expensive. One way to cut costs is to discuss with your printer employing colour on a limited number of pages. The correct terminology to use is 'forms' and refers to the number of pages that can be printed in one pass through the presses. A form could take 2, 4, 8 or 16 pages, perhaps more. For instance the front and back pages, say 1 and 8, of a publication will be passed through at the same time but pages 2 and 7 will not. So decide whether you want colour on the front and back pages.

Gatefolds

It is possible to produce a six-page or gatefold publication – these fold out to display three sides at a time. However, this is not a standard size and will cost more, but probably not as much as eight, which will require some form of stapling or stitching. It is also possible to insert extra single sheets but unless the publication is stapled or bound this may part company from the main publication. Should you decide to go down this route a feature could be made of the extra sheet, describing it as a bonus pull-out. But make sure nothing vital appears on it as it may come adrift.

There is a page limit in terms of logistics for many types of publication. An A5 directory which is simply stitched (stapled) will automatically spring open if too many pages are included (somewhere in the region of 60 sides is probably it). Progressing to a different format may add too much to the final bill but scaling up to an A4 version might solve the problem. A newspaper can look satisfactorily chunky but it may be worth making it appear more manageable by breaking it down into sections, much in the manner of weekend newspapers and their supplements.

Capacity is an important issue. Not only is postage becoming increasingly more expensive, but so is packaging and you should never stint on this. Publications of a longer-lasting nature such as directories or handbooks in binder format need specialist envelopes. The producer of the binder may well have thought of this and can provide specially designed and sized card box containers; these will add to the post bill but the contents will remain pristine. Weight could be kept down through the use of padded envelopes; it is worth doing a test run as these can also be pricy. Also protect sharp or well-defined corners on any publications as these can often work holes in even the toughest of padding.

When producing a newsletter, newspaper or magazine the envelope or polythene wrapper in which it is to be sent needs to be large enough to accommodate the publication. A C4 envelope may not be large enough to take the A4 publication so go for gussetted envelopes or something larger – try a few for size.

Factsheets and A4 publications may be destined for extended use by insertion in folders and the like. Again check the folder will comfortably accommodate the publication – split sections do not look attractive. Folders can also be constructed with gussets to give more space. An A4 folder with contents will of course need a larger-size envelope to accommodate it.

Distribution is a boring but crucial issue. It should be the responsibility of someone in the internal communication department to ensure transportation of the finished item actually works. If your prized efforts are simply being dumped at depots, how do they get from there to the desktop or workspace? Postage to home addresses may seem a luxury but the extra expense does at least ensure arrival. Check, however, that the recipient will welcome receiving effectively work mail at home. Make sure also that you are working from up-to-date address lists as this too will save on waste and disappointment.

Logistical aspects can serve to deflect you from the most important factor – ensuring the chosen format suits its desired purpose rather than the postal service requirements. If you have just one critical message to get across to a lot of people very quickly, perhaps a leaflet might be an option. These can vary enormously in size but tend to be fractions of an A4 sheet – a d/l (as printers refer to them) is such a sheet folded to make six sides. If your subject matter is weightier you might size up to A5 which will still fit into a handbag and is in fact A4 folded in half.

Newsletters should be used where there is more to say on a more regular basis. They are most usually A4 format although some may still be produced in A5 but this has a slightly old-fashioned, parish church magazine feel to it. An A4 newsletter is in fact A3 folded in half and you can have as many pages as you like; however, remember that printers operate in multiples of four and you will get charged even where your copy only fills three sides. You can also play with the A4 format but use a gatefold, similar to the d/l leaflet; this is, however, what in less polite printer circles is called a 'bastard' size, so will cost more. You do not have to restrict yourself to standard sizes but it will help in a budgetary sense.

Magazines most usually appear in an A4 format but other variants are also possible including tabloid which you would normally reserve for a newspaper format. Newspaper publications for internal communication purposes are most usually tabloid; broadsheet is far too unwieldy and appears to have had its day in the wider world too. But rules are made to be broken; the author has seen an annual report in the form of a calendar.

The next chapter looks at broadcast media.

KEY POINTS TO REMEMBER

- Print can be costly – remember to factor in artwork, typesetting, proofs, etc.
- Order sufficient copies first time – extra print runs are costly.
- Check all copy before sending it to printers.
- Proofread at each stage – mistakes do creep in.
- Use standard proof correction marks.
- Paper is expensive; check weight on postage costs.
- White paper with black print is still the easiest combination to read.
- Use tint panels sparingly; check how colour choices work on black and white photocopying.
- Select typefaces according to readability.
- Keep numbers of typefaces to minimum.
- Use inside covers for copy to keep costs down.
- Use colour photography sparingly for economic reasons.
- Make sure envelopes and other packaging are large enough for contents.

17

Broadcast – do it yourself or call in the experts?

Want to get something across quickly in an emergency? Visual imagery in the form of a video might be the answer. It works best when its full potential for engaging the audience is realized and so will work particularly well for major events and launches. Few organizations regard video in quite the same way as print and so it is unlikely to be used for everyday communications.

Should you think about it a little more deeply you will begin to realize that broadcast is probably going to be the most expensive way to reach your audiences in terms of set-up and production times.

As with print the most critical factor is in fact the content of your video. To make sure you do not stray over budget establish the key messages you will wish to transmit and then determine the way in which you plan to make these engaging. Much as with print publications, case studies – life in practice – are what grip rather than talking heads by the dozen.

Nowadays the hot money is on DVDs as the media that will overtake and replace video. This newer kid on the block provides an extra element – interactivity. It is also relatively cheap to produce discs (but not the content) that can be fed straight into desktop computers for one-to-one presentations. Equally these can be used on a departmental DVD player for team presentations.

It also seems to have overtaken another technological wonder of recent years – webstreaming. Few organizations are concentrating their efforts on straight to desktop. DVD discs take up very little capacity on the hard drive of the individual's computer whereas webstreaming will require rather a lot more. Although the gigabytes are becoming ever cheaper there are probably more efficient and appropriate uses for such 'space' than a special rallying cry to the troops.

According to a specialist video producer's website, video can be produced for as little as £1,000 a minute. You should realize it is unlikely you would get all that much for that money.

Writing in her guide to charity public relations, Moi Ali (1999) warns that it is not a matter of pointing a digital camera and simply downloading the contents. For the results to be worthwhile it can take months of careful planning and expertise and editing.

However, if you have plenty of time to get it right and the right set of skills on board, broadcast media, like its external cousins, will grab the attention like no other media. Very few organizations will have a spare cameraman on the staff and an editing suite on the premises. This is not territory for the amateur no matter how gifted. It is costly, but if video can be clearly argued to be an essential part of your communication mix then you can justify its share of the budget.

CELEBRITIES – HOME GROWN OR REAL?

Do not let your expert bamboozle you. Be very clear as to what you want to achieve and just who should be taking part on the action side of the camera.

In these days of Pop Idol and reality television there will probably be keen performers within your workforce both at the top and at other levels. Whether you should employ their skills is another matter. What is critical is to determine the script and whether or not they are the people to deliver it. Just how well respected and received are your would-be presenters among the key audiences? The receptionist is no doubt known to one and all, but is she the right voice for serious news?

Is your production a one-off or will you be putting out regular broadcasts? If frequency is critical, you may be well advised to get your amateur key presenters trained. At the very least they need to practise delivery of their scripts and how to use the kind of autocue that keeps much external media flowing on air. A trial recording will also show how voices sound on broadcast – sometimes quite different from their usual face-to-face settings.

And it is not just sound that counts: so does image. A bad hair day will be magnified on screen, thereby distracting from the key messages. Checked suits, stripy shirts, busy patterns and lurid ties may also play havoc with the viewers' eyeballs.

Although it may be fun and useful in terms of engagement and team building, if time is critical it may be safer to restrict in-house guest appearances to the minimum. News presenters and the like may come at a hefty premium but they are at least the consummate professionals and will deliver to time and on script. An added bonus is their familiarity with the audiences.

A word of warning, however. A young, rather flippant car show presenter may not be the one to deliver hard, financial messages unless of course you are in the racing industry or something similarly high octane.

Talking heads, whether it be the CEO or a celebrity, can become tedious so offset such footage by interspersing it with relevant site shots or better still action as buildings themselves can become boring.

Broadcast in this chapter also extends to audio tapes and dial-in services. Here physical appearance will not get in the way, but it is vital you ensure your speaker enunciates clearly. Think of the way you react to garbled messages on train tannoys on the way to and from work. If your audience literally cannot understand the message, how can they gain anything from it? Should your employee team be made up of a proportion of people who do not have English as a first language, translation or subtitles may be the answer.

In fact this is another area in which DVD will score over video, especially for organizations with a large overseas presence. You can run up to 32 different subtitle tracks, thus extending the reach of your presentation as necessary.

When filming, be prepared for a massive amount of standing around waiting for something to actually happen. Setting up lights seems to take positively ages. Filming schedules, especially those involving external footage, need to take account of Britain's notoriously fickle weather. You will be charged for downtime – so alternative schedules for inside filming will assist here.

If you have chosen to shoot indoors, pay attention to what is behind your speaker. It has been known for a mischievous cameraman to leave plant pots and worse apparently sprouting from the head of the presenter. A section on health and safety will not, for instance, be enhanced by scene-setting shots with rubbish piled against emergency exits featured in the background. Paying attention at this stage should save having to shoot more footage than necessary. The film crew, whether internal or external, needs to be well briefed but also accompanied to smooth over those little local difficulties.

Brief your 'actors' well. There is nothing more calculated to surprise and perhaps terrify the TV or radio novice than the length of the script needed to deliver just a few minutes of activity.

Along with interviews and panning shots of attractive interiors and exteriors you may also want to add music. If this is the case ensure you have the appropriate permissions and pay any fees required.

With today's digital cameras there may be a temptation to save money and do everything in-house. But this newest technology may not produce much better results than the VHS (Video Home System) that many of us may still rely on. A video recorded in the VHS format will not produce good enough quality – Betacam is the minimum standard to aim for.

WORKING WITH THE PROFESSIONALS

Production companies, like many other specialists, have their own language and it is important to make them translate what they are saying into your terminology. If they cannot or will not, move to one that can.

Your budget should include pre-production – research, story outline (or synopsis), preparation, story boarding (running order) and scripting. In addition, post-production needs to be factored in and include offline or rough (first) edit, online (final) editing, adding graphics, sound, voiceovers, credits and titles. Copying and packaging needs to be included. You may also want to produce printed support material.

Copyright is a major issue, and not just when it concerns someone else's music, graphics or images. Make sure the video's own overall copyright belongs to your organization. This should mean all material including that which ends up on the cutting room floor – otherwise some of your shots may well appear in someone else's video.

Contracts are important if you are dealing with outside presenters. Celebrities have been known to pull out of contracts – so build in clauses to counter this. It may also be worth having at least a couple of alternatives in mind for the worst-case scenario; this should spare your blushes and ease budget pressures.

Make sure too that you have signed consents where necessary. Customers and service users may decide to argue about their inclusion or the way the video has been edited after the event.

None of this has taken account of your own internal consent processes which are similar but more cumbersome than those that apply to printed material. Winning over those with the control of budgets is critical. Changing material late in the day is more difficult than for print and even more expensive. Should you be receiving funding from an external source it is also worth ensuring they are happy with progress and the results.

To find out more about video production pay a visit to the International Visual Communication Association website, details in Appendix 4.

KEY POINTS TO REMEMBER

- Video is expensive to produce; use for special purposes if budget is a major consideration.
- Go for real stories and ease up on the talking heads.
- Take the time to plan content.
- Build downtime into filming schedules especially in countries with unpredictable weather.
- Amateur footage is not an option; use the experts to shoot footage.
- Choose presenters from the audience's point of view.
- Make sure presenters speak clearly on camera.
- Check their wardrobe choices for the strobe effect.
- Make sure your locations are not distracting from or contradicting the message.
- Ensure all production stages are included in tenders and contracts.
- Check copyright issues.

18

Managing change

When a global company drifting towards the rocks realized it had to change, the internal communication manager did an unscientific but revealing study of its senior managers. She asked them how they managed internal communication in their part of the world. Here are some of their answers:

- I haven't got time.
- I'm trying to run a business.
- We're on e-mail.
- Don't they read the papers?

However, communication is the responsibility of the whole workforce, not just those towards the top. Communication is a three-way process: top down, bottom up and lateral, across functions. This chapter takes three case histories to highlight how three different organizations successfully managed the challenges of radical change with the three component parts of the tripod.

The first carried out a merger, the second sold off its European businesses and the third reorganized its operations to include outsourcing many of its operations to India.

But first some general principles on managing change. To start with, the management role. While employees do not expect to receive all their information from their managers the senior management role is crucial to success.

Most importantly, senior managers must own the messages they are delivering. If they pay lip-service then do their own thing, employees will soon find out and lose trust in the whole process. Next, they must be clear about what they can and cannot talk about. Commercially sensitive information, for example, will probably fall in the 'not' category. Managers should say why they cannot talk about such information for the time being. Nor should they speculate on what might happen. To speculate unsettles employees. Far from making employees feel they are on the inside track, speculation makes them uneasy.

Senior managers must also be encouraged to maintain communication, even if they have nothing new to say. That might sound odd, but in change situations employees need the reassurance that their managers are talking to them, even if only to explain how far they have got with the process.

Few managers are naturally comfortable with communicating face-to-face with their staff. Yet helping them do the job is not rocket science. It is a case of carrot and stick. The ideal carrot – and stick – is if the company recognizes communication as a core competence. If this is not a recognized – and rewarded – competence then the communication manager might like to start a conversation with the human resources professionals.

When BP researched what made a manager a good communicator, it came up with some surprising results. While perhaps 20 per cent related to natural talent and a similar percentage related to training, by far the most important aspect was the manager's attitude. Those who wanted to communicate were quite simply the best at it, including those who stuttered. So persuading managers that communication will help them deliver more effectively is one way forward.

If all else fails they can simply fake it. There is now a thriving industry in actors coaching managers to sound convincing, even if they do not feel it. It works, because success breeds success.

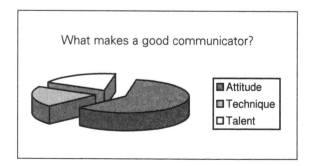

Figure 18.1   *What makes a good communicator – the characteristics needed to communicate effectively*

So far as the bottom-up part of the tripod is concerned, the one essential is for management to acknowledge they have received feedback and commit to action in a timely way. If they cannot act they must say why. Feedback tools are spelt out in more detail elsewhere in the book but useful ones include surveys, light-touch questionnaires, focus groups for an in-depth and qualitative understanding of issues, and the United States-style 'brown bag lunches'. With these a small group – frequently a cross-section of functions and seniority – sits down with a senior manager over a sandwich lunch. The manager's role is to listen rather than tell.

NETWORKS

Lateral communication is perhaps one of the most difficult to fix. How do you make sure that people in different units and functions and possibly different parts of the world are getting the same message in a sensible and timely way? Here is where networks play a starring role.

The communication manager mentioned at the start developed her first global network because she had to: she needed help. A key success factor for the network was the fact that she did not choose it. The relevant senior managers nominated and hence supported their representatives, not all of whom had communication experience. With this support the network was able to take decisions.

Other more informal networks arise out of similar needs. The group of people in different functions in head office, for example, who do not meet formally but recognize the work of those outside their departments impacts upon them. The discovery on a training session that several share a common interest. In one company, that led to a rock band being formed from staff around the world who went on to play in the Cleveland, Ohio Rock & Roll Hall of Fame.

Nor do networks need to meet frequently. Regular e-mails, telephone or video conferences help keep them alive. What they do need is a purpose and a skilled facilitator to make sure that people from different cultures, from head office to the regions, from one country to another, are fully involved in the decision making.

INTEGRATED COMMUNICATION

The merger

Creating appropriate networks was key for the merger between Glaxo Wellcome and SmithKlineBeecham. GSK's communication principles for the merger required that every task force, functional support team and special issue team should include a communications representative from each of the companies. Elaine Macfarlane, now Vice-President Corporate Internal Communications for GSK, set up a team of integration communicators with her opposite number from Glaxo Wellcome, Justine Frain. All communication had to be channelled through this extended team network to the interim executive planning committee. The respective CEOs of the legacy companies made the final decisions on what could – or could not – be communicated.

Elaine Macfarlane told a meeting of the Chartered Institute of Public Relations' Internal Communication Alliance that getting senior manager support and ensuring their visibility was crucial. 'Demand for information will be insatiable, so get your communication principles and guidelines established early', she said.

She also warned that the process would take longer than managers expected. She had to remind senior managers that although the merger had formally closed and stocks of the new company were trading, the merger was not over for employees. Far from relaxing on day one of the new company launch, it was essential to recognize that 'new' was not 'normal'. The company had to maintain merger-style communications during the transition into the new company communications structures and products.

A merger process needs to go through several phases, from denial to enthusiasm and from endings to new beginnings before it is complete and accepted (see Figure 18.2). Regular communication is essential. Where there was no new information GSK's senior managers reminded people of processes and timings and explained if necessary that certain decisions had had to be postponed.

People want to know what the change means for them. They want to know if they will have a job at the end of it. They want to know how they will fit into the new organization. Few of these answers will be known because they need to be worked out. So how do you handle demand for information that is not yet available? And what tools do you use as the organization progresses along the transition curve?

How you handle it partly depends on where you are on the curve. All change – good or bad – is unsettling and people will want lots of reassurance throughout the process. They will want someone to talk to. Upbeat graphs and statistics are not enough. So the primary tool of face-to-face communication will be particularly important at the start. People will want to hear 'the big picture' from senior management, compensation and benefits advice from their human resources professionals. The secondary tools – newsletters, videos and intranet – can carry the news and transition process updates and repeat and reinforce the key messages.

Transition curve

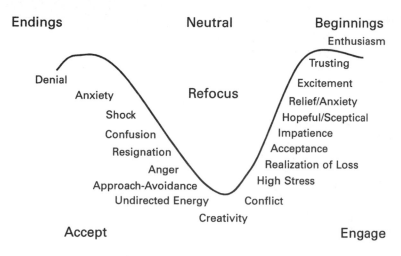

Figure 18.2 *The transition curve from denial to acceptance of change –
employees go through a large number of stages and reactions before they embrace
change* (Glaxo SmithKline)

Roadshows with senior management are best for explaining the big picture.
Their role is to paint a vision of the desired outcome. They are the credible
people to talk about why the organization had to change, why the particular
route was chosen, why it will be successful. That should be done at the
start.

Line managers are the natural and preferred source for information on
team goals and personal direction. When GSK established its communication principles and guidelines, it defined what the line managers could
credibly be expected to deliver in both their own and their team's eyes.
The company used other channels of communication such as the intranet
and e-mails for the rest.

So right from the start the line manager should commit to holding regular
meetings to give timely updates to employees on what is happening.
However, their role is as much about listening as telling. They will need to
be able to deal with the shock and anger. They are likely to need training
for this. You cannot fob people off with a printed handout, no matter how
glossily produced, while people are still going through the first part of the
transition process.

Where there is no new information – and while the big picture is being
filled in new information can be scarce – the line manager's communication
role will be as much about listening as telling. They can, however, remind
employees of the timetable for the transition, including when they can
expect to hear news about job decisions.

A word of warning here. Some line managers get so carried away with their communication role that they start telling their employees everything they hear, including rumours. You see this happening as the transition curve approaches the 'undirected energy' on the acceptance side. But it is counter-productive. As we said earlier in this chapter, speculation unsettles rather than comforts employees.

Throughout, the line management feedback role will be crucial. Line managers can evaluate and research issues as they arise and, in the case of a global organization, uncover the cultural nuances that can make or break a deal. Action taken on feedback helps make the transition from acceptance to engagement. Feedback should focus on:

- Is the message getting across?
- What do employees think of it?
- What is concerning people right now?

Training will help boost the confidence of line managers unused to communicating. It is also a good idea to provide line managers with a communication expert who can help, for example, anticipate questions and prepare answers.

As the organization progresses along the transition curve, the actions taken as a result of feedback will become more and more important. Employees will switch off if they feel they are not being listened to, so line managers need to be prepared to say what action has been taken – and what has not. If the result is no action then they need to say why not. It might, for example, be to do with commercial confidentiality, timing, or the simple fact that the senior management is not yet in a position to be able to give that information.

Primary face-to-face communication should be complemented and reinforced by whatever secondary tools are available, such as house magazines and the intranet. Some chief executives use a personal page on the intranet, or an e-mail 'from the chief executive', to reach out to all their employees with regular updates on what is happening. Feedback on specific issues will feature in these secondary tools.

New secondary tools may need to be developed, such as a dedicated merger video and newsletter. These tools enable a consistent set of messages to be delivered and can provide an ongoing reminder of why the merger is happening. Nothing shakes people going through the transition more than managers appearing to change their minds about what they have already said. If people lose trust in their managers the whole process can stall.

Communication consultant John Smythe (2002) makes the point that engagement is the 'process, considered or accidental, by which leaders and their employees become personally implicated in the performance of their own team in the context of contributing to a wider organisational change, strategy, transformation, operational improvement or day-to-day performance'. Effective communication, using both primary and secondary tools, will prepare the ground for engagement and help people see how all the elements of the change strategy fit together.

To return to the specific GSK merger, managing a merger for some 120,000 people in 130 countries involved balancing global, regional and national communications. The team of integration communicators not only helped track consistency of messages but also ensured coordination of sensitive issues that might unsettle its stakeholders – like, for example, planning to announce a site closure the same day as an analyst briefing forecasting high earnings. That was picked up by the team and the site closure announcement was delayed.

The sale

A very different operation, where timely communication was fundamental to success, was the decision of one European organization to sell off part of its business. This was spread across 10 countries and carried out by company employees and contractors. To add to the complexity it was not marketable as a whole because the potential buyers would be small businesses. It had to be kept going while it was being sold because if customers or employees were lost, the business became worthless.

The challenge for the communication strategy was to keep this diverse organization motivated. Here again the creation of the right networks helped. A network of communication managers across Europe supported the project team while a complementary network of human resources managers dealt with people issues and employment law. These two networks worked very closely together.

A second key success factor was the bonus plan set up for the business line managers. Reputation and people management were the main performance criteria.

The communication strategy had the following characteristics:

- Line managers to engage in frequent dialogue with staff and listen to staff concerns even if there is no news to tell them.
- Over-communicate news to those directly affected but under-communicate news to others; always communicate news via line managers.
- Give staff time to come to terms with one piece of news before delivering the next.
- Take full account of national/cultural issues and differentiate style and timing of messages in different countries.
- Manage the whole process with military precision.

Employees naturally asked why the new solution – the sale – should be any better than what had gone before. The emphasis on different options for different countries helped managers reply. It was not a 'one size fits all' approach and that helped local employees feel ownership of local solutions. There was also concern that announcements in one country would be seen as the 'writing on the wall' for other countries. However, early communication of the context – explaining the problems facing the business – helped give people time to get used to the need for radical change.

EU employment law requires pan-European consultation of cross-national business changes with significant social impact. Negotiating so many disparate local deals with a European Works Council would have been impossible. So general context was dealt with at European level, detail at local level.

Did it work? The business was sold, all staff were treated with dignity and the managers got their bonuses.

The reorganization

The final case history concerns Norwich Union Insurance (NUI) and the challenge it faced to improve performance a year after the company's merger with CGU (the insurance company formed from the merger of Commercial Union and General Accident). Interestingly NUI used a bottom-up approach to achieve success. They won the hearts and minds of the location and team managers first, rather than the top team, and created a groundswell to sweep away resistance to change.

While NUI had moved fast to rationalize structures, locations, products and systems to achieve the planned merger savings, it wanted to delve deeper to improve performance. At the same time the CEO started a culture change programme to move NUI from being a centrally controlled and internally focused organization to being an externally focused service provider.

Alastair Ham, NUI's Director of Organisational Development, master-minded the project. He is a fan of the Warner Burke/George Litwin causal model of organizational performance and change. This makes clear that sweeping strategic, structural and process changes is unlikely to deliver improved performance unless your people are motivated.

'Companies can never demand loyalty and motivation from their employees,' he says, 'they have to earn it from every individual they employ and that's not easy when job security can no longer be taken for granted.'

Working with Cathryn Riley, then NUI's Operations Director, he researched the local work unit and communications climate. (Riley is currently CEO of NUI's Healthcare business and IT Director for the Life business). They found that, like other organizations going through change, NUI's managers were largely out of touch with their staff. They spent more time filling in spreadsheets or doing project work than leading and communicating with their teams and centrally NUI was bombarding people with all sorts of irrelevant and confused information.

'We needed to put managers back in a position of leading their teams', says Alastair Ham.

Starting with the supportive managers involved in the research phase they asked them to conduct a daily 'huddle'. The idea was to focus on the performance of the team, provide relevant communications for their jobs and encourage them to raise any issues that were getting in the way of them doing what was asked.

Using external consultants they prepared the ground by making sure the 200-or-so staff and around 20 managers were up for it. Preparations for the managers culminated in a two-day offsite event with actors and an expert behavioural coach to equip them for what was to come.

'Managers had to get up from behind their desks and genuinely lead their teams and they had to resolve an absolute flood of issues, many of which were relatively trivial hygiene issues (ie to do with their working environment) but these were the things that mattered most to staff. Criteria for success was that it should be cost neutral, it should not damage performance and staff and managers would love it so much that they'd never let it be taken away' says Alastair Ham.

Each part of the business had to be won over – pull not push – and Alastair Ham's team used posters, competitions, intranet sites, staff diaries and humorous sketches acted by staff and managers at conferences. When the CEO heard about it he became one of the project's biggest supporters.

'True change does not happen just because the CEO says so', says Alastair Ham, 'but there's no doubt it helps.'

Mergers, changing distribution patterns and moving work to India meant NUI has had to manage situations where people were unfortunately due to lose their jobs. While giving people a financial reason to stay plays a part, it does not guarantee performance or attitude. Treating people with respect is essential and for NUI that means:

● allowing local managers to manage the situation;
● tapping in to everyone's pride and competitive edge by making performance standards clear and achievable;
● engaging them in how to make the changes happen;
● listening to concerns and issues.

The daily huddles have proved an ideal vehicle for all these things. Quarterly staff surveys show quarter on quarter improvements despite the uncertainty and difficulties facing people. Success is measured according to whatever the individual huddles are focusing on from sales and productivity to cash collection and customer satisfaction. All NUI managers get quarterly reports from their teams on how well they are doing across a number of critical factors believed to have most impact on performance.

Key to success in India has been making sure NUI measures the right things. With customer service in the UK much is implicit and taken for granted. In India, where staff are already very performance and customer focused, NUI has spelt out some of these implicit drivers, developed a clear and specific set of customer satisfaction measures and coached the teams how to achieve them.

Alastair Ham says they have had most success where NUI has combined a series of changes. Where they have been less successful is where they have been inconsistent, setting expectations about engagement in change that are not met. He says that in his experience internal communications departments tend to place their focus on corporate communications vehicles and are not skilled in organizational effectiveness and change. Where a change goes against the prevailing mindset, presentations and performance statistics do not win hearts and minds.

KEY POINTS TO REMEMBER

- Hear it from the boss face to face.
- Commit to regular meetings.
- Set up networks.
- Don't speculate.
- Act on feedback.
- Communicate, communicate, communicate.

19

Signposting the ether

They do keep saying paper is on the way out in terms of publications. Just in case this turns out to be true this chapter looks at some of the ways to make e-communications – communications without recourse to paper and ink – as effective as possible.

Referred to in some circles as electronic media or in certain academic quarters as computer mediated communication (CMC), it is important to remember that computers purely serve as the platform and should not be seen as the driver. Having a deep knowledge of HTML (hypertext mark-up language) and its successors is rather like assuming a typesetter can be entrusted with filling the pages of a newspaper and magazine with content. Today's more user-friendly packages should give the upper hand to the content providers rather than the technician; it is up to us to grasp the opportunity.

This chapter will not look at mark-up languages and the like – there are courses and other books that clearly do that very well – but will concentrate on what is needed from the technology to make for a better experience at the interface with the audience.

The previously separate concepts of reader, listener and viewer appear conflated as it is possible to be or do all three and add in a fourth – participant, or even a fifth – co-author. One aspect CMC does add to the mix that other vehicles necessarily struggle to provide is interactivity. This does, however, have to be designed in, not being completely automatic. But polls, pop-up menus and the like serve several purposes including developing and maintaining involvement, increasing interest and maximizing feedback.

E-MAIL – GETTING IT RIGHT

Before looking at ways to make intranets deliver on their promise most effectively, let us take a brief look at e-mail. With fewer opportunities to cluster around the water cooler, people see e-mail as a way of keeping the more informal organizational conversation going.

Because the technology gives the appearance of speed it can provoke expectations of instant responses; these have to be managed and the flood turned down to a smooth flow. Along with policies on what can or cannot be sent in terms of content, many companies are now setting frameworks for timing. Some have resorted to banning the use of e-mail on a given day of the week, forcing employees back to talking physically to their colleagues face to face. Other companies have also banned the sending of text messages and calls to mobile phones outside specified normal working hours. This is not necessarily universal practice however, but it is worth considering alongside policies on e-mail usage with outside bodies and the ways in which the internet can and cannot be surfed in company time.

Even innocent e-mails can be barred entrance because their titles contain a word deemed inflammatory. The word 'seduction' recently halted the progress of a romantically intended advertisement from a major florist chain in the run-up to Valentine's Day. Try to be short and snappy, but not to the point of confusing the issue.

If your e-mail address does not include your actual name, select one that does or use the subject header to make it clear who it is from. Some organizations insist on a communal inbox so use the same trick if you are writing to info or admin instead of a named individual.

We all know how we respond to carelessly addressed junk mail – a practice aim at the nearest waste paper bin. If you know the individual's name, use it in a salutation. Whether you address them formally as 'Dear Joe', more informally as 'Hi Joe' or just 'Joe' is best judged by company or individual preference. Some group mails where the recipients are all known to each other and regularly exchange such missives may ignore this stricture.

The overuse of capital letters or other extremes such as bold annoy people as it is regarded as the equivalent of shouting. Turn the 'cap lock' off.

Sloppily put-together publications irritate, and it is the work of a moment to spell check and also proofread your missive. The recipient will not automatically put in whatever it is you have missed out.

Just because it takes only a second to send a request or a question does not mean the recipient will be able to respond straight away. Give them time and take time yourself to read through the information.

E-MAIL – GETTING IT WRONG

In his book on e-public relations David Phillips (2001) sounds warning bells on a concept he dubs 'porosity'. This relates to the passage of information from within an organization to external audiences, outside the controlled and formal information flows and without regard for the broader consequences of the communication. This could be seen as the 21st-century version of whistle-blowing but it could equally be sheer inability to get to grips with the complexity of the computer. That is how he regards many 'leaks' which could have been made with relatively innocent intention. In other cases the sheer simplicity of the 'forward' icon has led to devastating disclosures.

Phillips uses the example of attaching a tender document to emphasize a point aimed at the recipient alone without realizing it can be sent or intercepted by an unintended audience. That person may possess or have access to other information, may put two and two together and make four for once. In other words the tender document might indicate plans to move to a different site heralding job losses. Of course this could in fact be at an early stage but you can see how screaming headlines in the mass media are made. So be aware that any e-mail message may end up in the wrong hands and think carefully before you word it and send it.

Intentional information sharing, which can be termed rather more positively as transparency, has always happened. Now it is simply quicker and easier to do at the click of a button; it also reaches further faster – around the globe even.

Messages can start on newsgroups, jump to online news media, broadcast media, politicians and all continue to add to the story so an innocent sharing of a media release or statement can have unforeseen repercussions.

Spam was already a problem back in 1998. It can deflect from important stuff that staff should be reading and can include unsolicited commercial e-mail. However, it is just as likely to be an internal version by which staff members or customers can share what they view as a joke but which could well be regarded as obscene and lead to a raid by the Vice Squad.

Disaffected employees can also create their own material which can serve to clog the system. They can also intentionally or otherwise introduce viruses.

Security aspects mean that companies can now use software to monitor staff e-mail to ensure certain information does not get out, but data protection legislation suggests it is at least good manners to let them know they are being monitored. It is worth bearing in mind that e-mail is not secure without encryption.

E-mails by their very nature are usually one-to-one communications. They can be used to send red alerts about critical issues – for instance Stock Exchange-sensitive information. Here security aspects are certainly crucial.

In terms of appearance, e-mails most closely resemble old-style memos but with the added informality of the telephone call minus the intimacy of the voice element. Appropriate forms of address and other 'etiquette' or 'netiquette' have not yet been fully determined. However, it is good practice to encourage staff to exercise a little caution, as the box panel sets out below.

E-MAIL ETIQUETTE – A FEW POINTERS

- Carefully word subject heading, or risk it being returned.
- Make it clear who the message is from.
- Do not 'cc' everyone, unless essential.
- Do provide a salutation (Dear Joe/ Hi Joe).
- Do not use solid banks of capital letters – it is not only rude but difficult to read.
- Check for mistakes and omitted words.
- Think twice before you send anything out.
- Think more than twice before you reply.
- Read everything you receive and send to the end.

TEXTING – BOTH PRO AND CON

Similarly text messaging is another way of getting time-sensitive information across and can be used to trigger cascade briefings.

Bob Schukai, Director of 3G Products Motorola, asserts that 3G or third generation technology can be used to generate more light-hearted communication. The sending of images may have a serious use in some quarters – sending back pictures of villains from the scene of a crime – but at the moment the emphasis is on getting individuals to use the technology in the first place.

The technology enables everyone not just to talk but also to see each other and exchange material. 3G makes it all faster, saving time all round. It is now possible to download sports highlights as the size of the screens and quality of image has improved sufficiently.

Video conferencing is made possible in miniature. A video message can be sent from Motorola's Europe sector vice-president and highlights can then be downloaded to the phone. Staff have also made their own mini videos to help demonstrate the capability of the new technology. 3G can handle much larger files at reasonably decent rates, with speeds six or seven times faster than the usual modem.

A key factor to bear in mind with mobile phone communication is that the messages need to be shorter than ever. Think *Sun* newspaper headlines or at the most the story intro, and cut in half. Do not, however, assume your audience is proficient in text English and use full words where possible.

WINDING UP THE INTRANET

Rather more flexibility and scope is offered by the intranet although again the luxury of broadsheet newspaper-length paragraphs are probably not an option. However, intranets have been with us for some years and the heady days of stripping copy to bare bones are over. Context is back, although more than likely in the form of links from the main copy.

You may also be responsible for the intermediate step to the outside world: extranets which link in larger groups that connect with other organizations involved in your work or as suppliers. Some regionally dispersed organizations such as the charity Sue Ryder Care have found it easier to set up an extranet to keep everyone in touch.

Intranets, extranets (intranets which involve suppliers and the like as well as employees) and websites all share an important feature – the endless opportunity to store background information to be retrieved only when needed. The hard copy's advantage is the information is all there, and the reader does not have to make a special effort to retrieve it. Not all users of intranets will have the technological experience to go and look for themselves, and this needs to be borne in mind. The process of retrieval either needs to be made very easy or training should be given.

According to David Phillips (2001) the theory is that the intranet will give every employee access to the same knowledge – they can conduct research and can study their own records. But in his view most intranets are not like this. Often they are masses of difficult-to-reach information which have not been designed to follow the way work is done in practice.

Firewalls installed for security reasons can end up preventing access. But wily staff can find ways round firewalls, so making important information hard to protect. It is rather better to limit the number of firewalls to those that are strictly necessary. Another theory sometimes more honoured in the breach is that employees should be able to create their own pages if they wish, thereby facilitating sharing of knowledge. You do, however, need

169

to keep a watchful eye on them as inappropriate material may find its way online.

Specialist consultancy Etribes, talking at an e-publishing conference held by the National Council for Voluntary Organizations in 2002, reckons that a whole library can go online in the form of newsletters, research papers, fliers, leaflets and directories. Provided the document is not a work in progress the pdf format is preferable because it cannot be easily altered in the same way that you can change Word documents.

The company estimated that costs of placing material online is around one-hundredth of normal distribution costs, stripping a postal direct mail bill of £312 to £437 per 1,000, down to £3.12 to £4.37 via e-mail. Online material can also be got out much quicker.

It is now much easier to take account of disabled members of the workforce as Braille formats are possible, but in order to ensure other employees do not have to go through the same often lengthy processes, these individuals should have their own dedicated version.

More people can be involved in content production but you do need to consider copy flow management – who will edit, and who will check copyright. Just because you fancy an image you saw online does not mean you can use it without charge or attribution.

Make use of all the organization's media to promote use of each other. The appearance of a print publication can often serve to prompt a surge of activity on the corporate website and, where it exists, e-mail forum.

Remember it is good practice to ensure consistency of image presentation across website, intranet and presentation materials.

WRITING ONLINE

Malcolm Davidson of Writing for the Web, speaking at the 2002 NCVO conference, shared the following points on effective online writing. See the panel opposite.

You can regard your intranet as the magazine or newspaper of the organization, combining extra elements from broadcast media such as clips. To exploit fully the potential you need to make yourself aware of the specification of the equipment your recipients are using. Flashes and moving graphics may not be viewable on certain systems and certainly will not be favoured by people with sight problems. Provide well-explained site maps to guide everyone in and out of your site.

WRITING FOR THE ONLINE AUDIENCE

- People read web pages 25 per cent slower than print.
- They scan the visual elements and skim read the content.
- Less than 10 per cent will scroll the pages.
- Headlines are more important than pictures.
- Low resolution and screen flicker can affect reading.
- Make text easily scannable by breaking into chunks and linking to other pages.
- Make copy brief.
- Use frequent headlines, subheads, navigation and hyperlinks to break it up.
- Make the content really attractive in itself.
- Get to the point fast when writing for the screen.
- Hone every word, sentence and paragraph.
- Format text for rapid scanning.
- Provide readable case studies with interesting photographs.
- Avoid colour conflicts and distracting elements.
- Do not use reverse white out of black or colour.
- Use readable fonts, sizes and styles.
- Cut line length to no more than 10 words.
- Do not use too many capital letters, italics or unusual typefaces.
- Do underscore hyperlinks, give links summaries so people know what they are.
- Use bold, bullet points, numbering, indentation to make text stand out.
- Take a tip from newspapers: do not run copy on below the fold (below the screen).
- Break lengthy articles into no more than A4 page lengths.
- Restrict copy to no more than two pages or 500 words.
- Offer opportunities to download pdf, Word file or e-mail to a friend.

GETTING THE CONTENT RIGHT ONLINE

Speaking at the Volcom Conference for the voluntary sector in 2004, Content and Code provided an intriguing list of engaging content augmented with a few extra suggestions as outlined in the box below.

WHAT MAKES A GOOD READ

- news;
- policies;
- procedures;
- office/region directory;
- application forms;
- reports;
- publications;
- online training;
- FAQs;
- weather;
- news (feed to actual newspapers);
- travel sites;
- calendar;
- staff directory;
- profile pages on staff;
- personalization;
- discussion boards (not just work, also *Eastenders*/latest reality show);
- work portal – integration;
- interactive training;
- e-commerce – stationery/ordering;
- the canteen menus;
- acronym/jargon-buster;
- integrated e-mail;
- instant messaging;
- health and safety matters;
- dictionary;
- corporate catalogue;
- small ads (for sale/swap items);
- project management programme;
- bottom-line figures.

Content and Code believe that to be truly effective an intranet needs to be the one good, true, reliable source for all staff so it must be the most up-to-date with the latest version of expenses forms and policies. To do this documents must be stored centrally and not hidden away on the author's computer inaccessible to anyone else.

There is an argument for decentralized control with internal audiences empowered to put in content. So publishing must be as easy as printing a hard copy.

Code and Content say that building an effective intranet is all in the planning and in the consultation with all users. They suggest the requirements assessment can be done internally or by consultants, but should be treated seriously and take the form of workshops or discussion groups held with different parts of the organization.

Hosting of the site can be done in-house depending on the size of the organization, but probably not in the internal communication function itself. It can be outsourced.

The advantages of getting it right are that the organization should be able to cut direct costs, reduce printing and copying costs, cut directory enquiry-type calls, free up space and so reduce storage costs, and make other savings on network and administrative costs. Less obviously an effective intranet should increase productivity, save labour, improve internal procedures, cut back on duplication and waste and improve customer service.

Employees should be able to subscribe to new versions of documents, to search their file servers, search external sites as well as internal files generally, and subscribe to alerts to any changes. Booking forthcoming training online is also a popular option.

Designers should deliberately build up relationship networks across regional outposts. These more informal channels can be encouraged to flourish through the setting up of 'Poll of the week' – which may focus on such essentials as where to hold the Christmas party. It is vital that departments and useful information are just one click away. Employee profiles can explain who does what and reports to whom, providing an organizational tree.

Chasing copy is an eternal headache. The answer can be to give every document two owners – the author and their boss; that soon sorts out the deadline issue. But it can run the risk of not one but two people including changes, amending, altering and rewriting.

INTRANET OF RECORD

Print newsletters can be replaced to some extent by text e-mail newsletters. These obviously take less time to pull together and require little artistry in terms of layout. You will need to exercise your creative gifts on the words to ensure they are read.

The time set aside to read a newsletter online is probably no more and very probably less than most people devote to unsolicited postal junk mail. You can expand on your little gems through links back to the internal website, as attachments are not especially welcome.

To recap, to get the most communication juice out of the new technology follow the tips below.

MAKING THE MOST OF YOUR E-COMMUNICATIONS

- Cut your writing to the bone.
- Find out the average size of your recipient's screen and design your pages to suit.
- Check the level of technology at their end.
- Keep it simple.
- If you can't go flashy make your content punchy.
- Update your news regularly.
- Use all your media to promote the rest of the mix.

It is of course possible for companies to employ all the individuals necessary to do everything themselves but this is not a particularly efficient use of resources. In Chapter 21 we look at outsourcing all or part of the internal communication function.

KEY POINTS TO REMEMBER

- Computers purely provide the platform for communication – nothing more.
- Exploit the benefits of interactivity offered.
- See e-mail as just one tool in the communicator's war chest.
- Be careful of choice of heading for e-mail if you want it to arrive.
- Establish clear corporate policy on e-mail and internet usage.
- Check your messages before you send them.
- Be careful how you use the forward button to avoid sharing information indiscriminately.
- Word all e-mails carefully – someone else could share them around for you.
- Use texting for news flashes and alerts.
- Information in texts, e-mails and websites should be kept short.
- Make sure logos and images are consistent across all online and offline publications.
- Make intranets user-friendly with interesting and varied content; update them regularly.

20

How to measure success

An unattributed news item in the September 2003 issue of *Professional Manager* sounds the warning bell to all communicators. A study by researchers Intercommunic8 showed that 37 per cent of the 1,000 people polled felt that whatever they received in terms of communication failed to explain their organization's values. Few managers were regarded as more than average at communicating – sounds familiar?

For communication to earn its place at the boardroom table or at least the ear of the people in the rarefied upper echelons, how everything the communicator does impacts on the bottom line needs to be demonstrated.

In this chapter the world of measurement and evaluation is explored and given something of a human face by looking at some of the ways in which practitioners are actually running the ruler over organizational plans and activities.

Measurement can instil a certain amount of fear in the communications professional. This may be because figures, statistics and the like are not their natural territory, whereas words and less often images are rather more familiar. Perhaps it seems boring and complex, but every action has a financial cost which may appear to outweigh perceived benefits. With the right statistics to hand internal communications can demonstrate how it helps every other department (human resources, finance, *et al*) demonstrate benefits. In the past, failure to demonstrate an ability to add value has resulted in the function being at the head of the queue when budget cuts are handed out. Without good measures in place, arguing for a fairer slice of the cake is that much harder.

David Boyle (2001) makes the point that if you choose the wrong thing to measure you will get the opposite result or effect to what you wanted to achieve. Unclear wording on surveys may give no real clue as to why a particular programme is failing. Timing may be cited as the issue, but does that mean the time of day that an activity occurs, or the duration of that activity? Without clarity the numbers are meaningless.

Fear of measurement can also be the result of not understanding the mechanics. Looked at simply, evaluation can help you get where you need to be and plan the route map for the next stage on. For one thing is sure: there is a constant need to keep counting and taking soundings from the corporate depths.

David Clutterbuck (1997), writing in the *Handbook of Internal Communication* illustrates how you can measure at a number of levels including message, programme or campaign, channel/medium and environment. These can all be tracked and measured individually or collectively.

It is possible to measure both what are termed hard or soft, quantitative or qualitative measures. Hard measures would provide a strict number count – how many people actually read the publication. Soft measures might show how they reacted to particular items or to the publication overall.

Depending on budget, you can do this cheaply or expensively. Focus groups are likely to provide a wealth of detail but can be expensive to set up if done properly. Observation may seem a cheap option but it is hard to carry this out without drawing attention to the process and so affecting it.

Before getting out the calculator or the slide rule you will need to develop a clear understanding of where the organization aims to be in terms of market share and related factors. Presumably there are marketing statistics, accounts and the like; also external media coverage which will show external views on the company.

Top management should have a clear idea regarding their desired goals. Desk research will provide a starting point as it does for external research, but it is only as good as the information stored. It can at the least be used to establish which aspects of the internal communication programme need extra attention.

The lessons for professional communicators would appear to be that there are lots of different things to measure out there. Do you measure them all or do you decide which ones are important and relevant? For what reason are you measuring them? What is going to happen to the information you collect and how will it be used?

BENCHMARKING

In the lead-up to a major internal survey it can be useful to look around for other organizations of similar size, complexity, business interest and/or geography to act as a counterbalance. Benchmarking can be an invaluable tool, not just a one-off measurement, and is at its best when used to encourage continuous improvement. It should be used over time and if not continuously at least at previously agreed stages.

Although communication is obviously vital there are other factors that may be having an even greater impact on performance. When looking for evidence of its impact it is better to select a few key points to explore rather than attempt to solve all problems in one go.

Internally it may be possible to measure the performance of one department against another, especially where there is evidence that all other things being equal (communication channels, vehicles, content) one is outperforming the other. To produce meaningful data the measures used would have to be pertinent to both – perhaps client contact and client satisfaction.

Not everyone agrees there is a value to benchmarking. Cable & Wireless found it difficult to find appropriately sized or dispersed organizations to measure upto, so decided to benchmark only against itself. Katie Hadgraft, UK Internal Communications Manager, believes that benchmarking can lead to complacency.

She says its Voice of the Employee survey enables the company to 'establish past performance in order to move forward more effectively. We check each wave to see if actions have been successful.'

Technology can be used to facilitate the whole process. There are online measurement tools which can deliver results instantly and in other languages if necessary. A key success factor in all internal investigative work is to use simple language.

SURVEYS

Readership surveys and panels can be used to gauge the success of overall efforts and as a starting point for further more in-depth research.

Surveys are not necessarily at the cheap end of research, although technology is helping to bring down the cost. They are probably the most common way of gauging the organization's temperature and can be delivered by telephone (potentially costly in time and money) or hard copy and posted, or online. The whole staff group or a representative proportion can be used as a sample.

Surveys can be short and sweet or very long and involved. If you are simply testing reaction to your new version newsletter a 'quick and dirty' tick-box sheet may do the trick admirably. However, if you are wanting a broader view you might opt for page upon page of questions. Just who will be collecting and then analysing the statistics for you? If you have a specialist on board get their help. Surveys can be conducted by an outside consultancy.

There is an inherent danger in satisfaction surveys that the organization will not be able to act on what it learns and the upshot will be a thoroughly disillusioned workforce. If you are not going to be able to deliver what is asked for, the most sensible thing to do might be not to ask those specific questions in the first place. This may seem largely a matter of concern for human resources, but internal communications practitioners might find the issue has to be addressed through the organization's communications vehicles.

After a short time producing and looking at evaluation sheets (which are after all simply a snapshot satisfaction survey) and more in-depth questionnaires you will come to learn what responses to expect. What on earth do you do with the statement that one speaker at an event kept pacing up and down, especially if you have no idea who they mean? However, you can do something about not sticking to the programme and not starting on time if those are the bugbears. It is important to be clear what you can have an impact on.

But if questionnaires are designed carefully and some thought is given to precisely what it is you are looking for, you may get back some very useful data. Using scales running from 1 to 5 with some clear guidance as to which end is good, and which end is bad, makes it far easier to spot areas for concern and therefore action. Questionnaires can have a communicative function of their own in that a loosely worded one will not only confuse but also suggest the organization does not really care and is merely going through the motions.

An over-reliance on numbers will take care of the quantitative end of things but omit the rich data which could provide the inspiration for future changes. So when designing questionnaires, allow respondents some opportunity to expand on their tick-box answers with fuller comments. It is also important to tell your informants about planned follow-up action.

To improve response, why not borrow a trick from the commercial world? If you are expecting people to give up valuable time to fill out your questionnaire, offer the chance to win a bottle of wine or some other appropriate prize.

So what can you measure?

Individual departments and the organization as a whole may need to measure factors such as job interest, promotion prospects, stress, status or confidence in management. The internal communicator will be involved to some extent in the delivery, the interpretation of results and communicating plans for corrective action.

When looking at internal communication itself you will want to measure what is directly attributable to the function, but give some passing reference to factors outside your control.

Those that you can affect include the following set out in the box below.

FACTORS COMMUNICATOR CAN INFLUENCE:

- Is the language clear?*
- How often does the publication appear?
- Can everyone access it?
- Do they understand the key messages?
- Is the material relevant?
- Could it be delivered through a different medium?
- Is the timing right?
- How will results and any follow-up action be communicated?

The Flesch Formula looks at the number of syllables in words and sentence length to determine difficulty. The Dale-Chall Formula takes account of average sentence length and the number of words that do not appear on a list of 3,000 common words. The Gunning Formula looks at rather more factors including average sentence length, number of sentences used, verbs, prevalence of abstract words and percentage of long words, among others. Fry comes up with an equation which works on the basis of selecting three 100-word passages which are then inspected to establish the average number of syllables and sentences to come up with an average reading age. For more on all the above see Cutlip, Center and Broom (1985).

Perhaps a much simpler way would be to establish which daily newspapers your chosen audiences read and then look to model your efforts on theirs. Sentences and paragraphs in the average tabloid newspaper appear to shorten at least every decade. No more than 32 words for the first paragraph according to the *Financial Times*, so if your publication is modelled on the *Sun* be prepared for a shock.

Simplify things for your respondents by using tick-box formats wherever possible. See a typical Likert scale in Figure 20.1.

How Cable and Wireless did it

The global company Cable and Wireless had like many others suffered from a glut of surveys, with different departments sending them out whenever

---

* Readability or keeping things simple is crucial when it comes to content. There are a number of tools available which will help gauge the readability of your content, sometimes called the 'fog index'.

	strongly agree	agree	neither agree nor disagree	disagree	strongly disagree
I receive enough information to do my job.	☐	☐	☐	☐	☐
I have no means of expressing my views to management.	☐	☐	☐	☐	☐
My supervisor/manager has good communication skills.	☐	☐	☐	☐	☐
My supervisor/manager keeps me regularly informed of the company's progress.	☐	☐	☐	☐	☐

Figure 20.1   *Likert scale – a popular tool used by researchers for testing shades of opinion*

inspiration struck. Those on the receiving end were showing classic signs of survey fatigue, especially as they did not always receive feedback.

It was decided to coordinate and concentrate survey activity, and Voice of the Employee was the result. For some time the company had been conducting an online customer satisfaction survey, Voice of the Consumer, and it was decided to align the two so that discrepancies in results could be acted upon.

Surveying the whole workforce, certainly a global one, is not to be undertaken lightly, so it was first piloted and was then gradually rolled out. A first snapshot of company performance was taken in one part of the organization by MORI.

As well as looking at performance aspects the survey was designed to find out what employees thought of their working environment. Questions were designed to establish their commitment, whether they worked well with their supervisors and whether there were any big issues that were stopping them performing. Questions were linked to key performance indicators and the responses to relevant questions used in assessment of senior managers' performance.

The company demonstrated action on receipt of feedback so essential for credibility with employees. So many members of one overseas-based team made adverse comments on their working conditions that they were relocated to more suitable premises.

Katie Hadgraft of Cable and Wireless describes Voice of the Employee as 'a change management tool for the company. It is changing the way senior managers interact with their people. It is starting to change behaviours within the company. The linkage work we undertake with Voice of the Customer is a particularly powerful way of correlating employee perform-ance against customer loyalty.'

Although conducted mainly online, in recognition that some field engineers do not have online access a print version of the survey was made available. The first survey attracted a 77 per cent response rate, the second 61 per cent.

Fifty per cent of employees selected randomly twice a year are surveyed anonymously. The survey is intended to give employees a formal voice by gathering insights and feedback in a regular, consistent and objective manner.

Survey pointers

Points to consider when embarking on surveys are outlined in the box below.

CHECKLIST FOR SURVEYS

- online or print;
- tell them why;
- decide on frequency;
- measure only what matters;
- phrase your questions clearly;
- use simple language;
- keep them succinct;
- have a firm deadline;
- give them the results.

The channel, whether online, print or telephone, will be determined by available staffing at the collection end but also should take account of the time and skills available to respondents. They need to know why you are suddenly taking an interest, and normal communication vehicles can help explain. Do not try to measure too much all at once. Use short, clear sent-ences or questions. Tell the respondents when you need their responses by, and when you expect to feedback results – and do it when you say you will.

So just how often should you be dusting down the thermometer to gauge the temperature of the organization? If the organization is relatively stable then perhaps quarterly or twice yearly might be fine. Yearly is likely to be seen as a major occasion and any less frequently than that could prove worthless as staff move on and other factors change.

However, if you are in the run-up to major change perhaps checking the temperature gauge almost constantly may pay off. Consultant Mark Winter (2002) reports that Prudential UK took soundings on a weekly basis during the run-up to major structural change.

This was done quickly and relatively cheaply through a random online survey which targeted different staff across the organization each week, thus overcoming that well known condition – survey fatigue. Questions covered understanding of the changes and responses to them. This showed how attitudes changed over a period from severe anxiety to relative calm.

AUDITS

Surveys are likely to be used to look at a wide range of issues which may or may not be causing concern to management and staff themselves.

Audits are becoming increasingly popular as internal communication is seen as a strategic tool. An audit is likely to be used to look in more detail at specific aspects of communications activity. Such a tool will look at channels of communication to identify where there may be communication 'black spots' or gaps, and at the media vehicles used.

There are a range of different audits that can be employed. PR audits are most likely to focus on issues around messages and whether or not you have targeted the right people. Production targets might be essential reading for the factory floor but seem largely irrelevant to the service centre.

Communications audits will relate to the effectiveness of channels and content. Technical issues may slow down channels which may be critical if information is needed straight away and choice and treatment of subject matter will also be of concern here.

Harder to gauge will be the results from social audits which will focus on the effects that communications are having on the chosen audience and the wider organization. These are likely to take time to deliver and interpret.

In-house staff are not always the right people to conduct such audits if the real world is to be captured in meaningful snapshot. These surveys are usually conducted by external consultants or at least with their help to ensure the anxieties of in-house practitioners do not affect results. They should also be more objective, which could be seen as a strength by the respondents. Reed in the *Handbook of Internal Communication* (1997) provides a wealth of material on audits.

Technology now makes it possible to run regular audits of communication vehicles. One high street bank uses voting systems to enable staff members of their communication audit teams to express their views regarding particular aspects. The results are instantly available to the communication practitioner who can then explore them further.

OTHER WAYS IN

Measurement does not have to be done in a completely formal manner. Readership panels can feed back essential data with a lot more background than can be elicited from cold questionnaires. This can take the form of focus groups which come together only once or twice, or they could be constituted to meet on a regular basis. Focus groups are expensive in time and labour terms, and need therefore to be designed carefully and facilitated by trained people.

Adding competitions to publications provides a useful feedback mechanism and you should be keeping an eye on letters pages and other forms of contribution. These devices are relatively cost-free apart from the occasional incentive and surprisingly popular.

LOOKING BACK AND ONWARDS

'Evaluation' is a word with as many interpretations as users. It seems likely that it is used interchangeably with other measurement terminology. It is used here to mean measurement of activity that has taken place and how it can be used to fine-tune practice for the future.

Speaking at the Internal Communication Alliance launch event in October 2002, CIPR Excellence Award finalist Seeboard referred to its practice of conducting evaluation at every stage of its branding project. It used questionnaires, focus groups, vox pops on its intranet, surveys and 'mystery shopper'-type activity whereby performance is tested without the employee being aware of the process.

A survey during the first phase showed 99 per cent understood the new customer vision. Separately, the twice-yearly staff survey attracted a creditable 83 per cent response rate. Some 88 per cent would apparently recommend Seeboard as a good place to work, 92 per cent felt proud to work for the company and 95 per cent knew the priorities of their team. All this was uncovered while Seeboard was being sold to the LE group.

While it can be difficult to demonstrate easily how it supports the bottom line, it could be argued that without effective internal communication there would be a negative impact in terms of the cost of failure, loss of valuable employees or of lost opportunity. One to bear in mind when you find yourself in the hot seat facing the finance director. An economic argument amply supported with forecast figures could demonstrate that staff need to know what is expected of them in order to deliver it – so failing to keep them informed would be costly.

A framework would give top management a clear understanding of what can be measured; a description of what is being measured at the moment;

recommending what should be measured in the future and also why and how, the cost and time scale – thereby giving an opportunity to choose between the options.

Simply producing the numbers – so many hits on the intranet, such and such a percentage of employees think or know a certain set of facts – is no longer enough. You need to add extra dimensions by looking for the reasoning behind the figures or at least provide some context. This is where qualitative information collected from more in-depth interviews would come in.

There needs to be an intertwining of both quantitative and qualitative approaches. Management tends to get distracted with the process end of research unless there is a clear explanation as to why something is being measured in a particular way, at a particular place and time.

Communicators find that kind of justification hard to deliver, but if they can develop the skills to do it they will be able to concentrate their efforts on what matters most – what the respondents are telling you.

Back in 1995 the ITEM group came up with a framework which still serves as a useful checklist for all evaluators. The consultancy believes that internal communication can be measured at four levels as the following panel indicates.

MEASUREMENT MATRIX

- Campaign processes: efficiency of planning and execution.
- Campaign outputs: did anything change?
- Media processes: efficiency of each medium.
- Media outputs: effectiveness of each medium.

KEY POINTS TO REMEMBER

- Measure the right thing, and not too many factors all at once.
- Qualitative and quantitative measures are not mutually exclusive – one provides depth, the other numbers.
- Benchmarking can set the framework for future plotting of the corporate course and its success.
- Start with desk research including internal statistics before seeking external clarification.
- Measure regularly – longer than yearly and it is historic and irrelevant.
- Make use of technology where possible to bring down costs.
- Simple feedback devices such as competitions can give a quick snapshot cheaply.

21

How to make it happen – gone shopping!

Even in the age of information technology the typesetter and other suppliers are not entirely superseded. Perhaps harking back to days when it was still possible to move from secretary to boss in the press office (a long time ago) there has been a tendency in some places to expect a good typist to be a good journalist, layout artist and photographer all rolled into one. However, if you want a decent end product consistently over time, do not venture down this route.

Even where there is a stand-alone function there has been an often misplaced belief in the magical all-rounder. Originally a newspaper and magazine journalist, the author never ventured into the darkroom.

After all, the professional photographer's skills do extend beyond the click of a digital camera and, if you are strictly honest, you will agree that unless you have a full understanding of lighting and composition in many cases your efforts will resemble holiday snapshots.

Industrial giants have been known to resort to the use of photo-booth snaps to plug those awkward spaces between words. Remember that old cliché about every picture telling a story and being worth a thousand words.

Both can be true if the picture is the right one for the job in hand, but are you sure you are the right person to take it and wield your pen at the same time?

This chapter will look at going shopping for those necessary services which, if well selected, will help convert you from delivery mode to strategist.

STARTING FROM SCRATCH

It is still possible to be given a clean slate on which to make your mark when taking up an internal communications role for an organization. But even if you have held down such a position for a long period it is worth being objective and questioning how things are currently done and whether they could be done at least differently, if not perhaps better by someone else.

Supposing you are the internal communication function in its entirety – what next? It is unlikely that you alone will be able to produce the ideas, the words, the images, the design, the printed page and then despatch it to the grateful reader. Intranets have consigned some of the above roles and tasks to the dustbin of history, but not all.

If your operation is likely to be of a sufficient size and complexity you could appoint your very own in-house based specialist and in Appendix 1 we talk about those specific tasks and skills. Here we concentrate on purchasing services.

As highlighted in Chapter 6 you can buy any service you want out there from licking and sticking stamps on envelopes, to taking the longer strategic view. To some extent whether you go down the route of outsourcing purely tactical support or the hard thinking depends on the skills base you have in-house and the existing demands on staff time.

Before deciding to hand over a large chunk of your budget to an outsider, first make an audit of what already exists in terms of skills and experience in order to identify true gaps. Should you need some no-nonsense advice tinged with years of experience, it may be worthwhile calling in a seasoned practitioner who will not mince words in the boardroom. They may not be saying things that are totally new to you, but the extra gravitas which they project may get those words heard.

However, if your relationship with those at the top of the organization is as you would wish, you may require extra resources for assistance with idea generation and then with breathing life into those ideas.

At one end of the spectrum communications consultancies have the skills on tap to provide one-to-one coaching for managers, and top ones at that, who need help in face-to-face communication situations, be they one-to-one discussions or groups needing motivation of a high calibre.

At the other end of the spectrum, consultancies can provide both the ideas and the technological know-how to refresh what you are doing, and to support inexperienced people in rising to meet a particular challenge such as a takeover or merger.

WHERE TO LOOK

To some extent this depends on what it is you are looking for. If you are planning to outsource elements of your publication programme you may be able to pick up names from the back pages of publications like *PR Week*. Perhaps a more effective approach is to collect in-house publications that you like the look of, see who is involved in the production and make the initial approach. A rifle through the filing cabinet or the departmental in-tray every so often will also more than likely turn up a few possibilities on this front.

Associations such as the Chartered Institute of Public Relations' Internal Communication Alliance and the British Association of Communicators in Business are worth joining to keep up to date with the communications world.

Strategic advice is probably going to be slightly harder work to track down in the first instance. Services such as the Chartered Institute of Public Relations' Matchmaker system should produce a shortlist. But it is worth taking your time over such purchases. No doubt you are reading appropriate publications (for inspiration see References and Further Reading sections) and it could be fruitful to extend this into the human resources field and read a little more widely. Take a note of interesting case studies and add the consultants concerned to your personal long list.

Recommendation by word of mouth is often regarded much more highly than a cold-call approach. Keep up your contacts with similar-level practitioners not just in your industrial sector but in others too, and check out the names that have impressed. Write-ups in the trade press or academic journals, particularly those authored by the consultants concerned, may not tell the full story – get the other side from those on the receiving or paying end.

If the budget will stand it, attend a few industry events; there are sure to be consultants present. Look out for your favoured names on speaker lists – not only will you get to see and hear them in action, you may be able to spend time with them afterwards.

Should you be operating in the public or voluntary sector it is regarded as good practice to advertise major tenders. This may sound tedious and long-winded but it can bring in some interesting outsiders you may not have considered. Advertisements for these usually follow a strict format which may not offer much scope for creativity but does mean it should be possible to compare like for like among those responding.

The advertisement in these cases is possibly the easiest item to produce; the important aspect is the tender specification document which can run to many pages. The structure may seem cumbersome and possibly unnecessary in its scope and detail but it can provide a framework for an effective briefing document to be prepared. Seek advice from your procurement department when preparing the tender.

PREPARING THE BRIEF

So you have identified your targets and want to approach them. Fine-tuning the briefing document should ensure your effort is rather more rewarding than fishing in a paddling pool instead of the proverbial fish farm. Any such document should include a fair amount of background on your organization and ought to include the items listed in the panel below.

THE CONTENTS OF THE BRIEF

- mission of the organization;
- goal of the IC programme;
- industrial sector;
- size of organization – staffing, financial;
- where employees are based (UK, overseas);
- any specific issues, including language difficulties;
- parent organizations;
- internal communication activities already under way;
- timescale (when needed, how often, how long for);
- expected results;
- responsibility for production;
- budget.

Add items such as existing publications, annual reports and media cuttings as background to the main briefing document. In these days of websites galore it may seem that much of this should be unnecessary and that the experienced consultant will know where to look in terms of their own research. There is an element of truth in this and consultants can be pointed in the direction of the corporate website to collect back-up material. However, it is worth being prepared to offer the paper-based versions of anything available online and important documents that are not.

There is a rather more fundamental temptation with websites, which is to rely on these and to fail to produce a briefing document of any real substance. Providing a well-considered and clear document will save time at later stages of the pitching process. Unless you are clear on your objectives for the programme you are likely to have to wade through a lot of irrelevant material. Without that clarity on your own behalf you will be offered off-the-shelf approaches which may bear little relationship to your specific problem.

You may be impressed by the speed at which consultants respond to your brief. This may appear to indicate a capacity to hit deadlines – obviously critical. But there is some truth in the old saying 'more haste, less speed' – a more thoughtful approach might deliver better results. So build in sufficient time to the initial process for consultancies to respond – probably no more than three to four weeks. Much less that that and you may receive a rather rushed response or none at all.

At this early stage be prepared to take questions by telephone or e-mail from interested parties but do not agree to too many meetings. Treating each and every approach in the same manner is equitable to all. A failure to ask questions on the part of a consultant at this stage does not mean they are inadequate – perhaps your briefing document has done its job as required. If, however, you are repeatedly asked the same questions, why not send out a FAQs (frequently asked questions) document to all respondents.

INTERVIEWING LIKELY CONTENDERS

Once the pitch documents are in, give yourself sufficient time to consider all proposals, marking them against a rating system to ensure all your points are covered. Hopefully you have not been seduced by the idea of the immensely long list – six at this stage is quite sufficient. By all means follow up documents with further questions to consultants, but now prepare for the actual pitching process. You should have been able to reduce the long list to a short list of three, certainly no more than four. Have a clear date in mind and set aside the whole day to carry out the process. Make sure there are no interruptions, and switch off mobile phones.

Recruiting a consultant is very like recruiting an individual in some respects, and should be treated with as much care and courtesy. Ensure your diary and those of others involved on the interviewing panel are clear of other distractions. Prepare questions that are common to all but also specific to the proposal being examined. Where possible give the date of the interviews in the briefing document – there is nothing more frustrating for a consultant than having to pull out having carried out so much work in advance.

A special word here if you are requiring a major demonstration of creative ideas and process: be prepared to provide a fee. Many internal and external communications consultancies are now tired of spending so much of their time and resources with no obvious return. For many, work put in at the pitch stage will constitute anything up to a third of the thinking and doing required to produce the end product.

Allow a good-sized time slot for each presentation – perhaps 90 minutes – and give yourself and others on the receiving end a clear period in between to be able to approach each presentation afresh. It is bad manners to keep applicants waiting and very bad form for them to be sharing the same waiting space.

Provide the requested technology for the pitch – data projectors and the like – and make sure they work. Conduct the meetings in a good-sized room with comfortable furniture and sufficient refreshment. Keep the 'judging panel' to a reasonable size – three is good as a casting vote is automatically built in to break any potential deadlock. Divide up the questions according to the questioner's own background and make sure all necessary questions get asked.

Make your decision quickly and do not request return visits – it all costs money. Keep all those who participated informed of the details of the process and of your decision in the timescale promised. Silence communicates rudeness and could well be hurtful to your organization's long-term reputation.

As with external relations consultancies, be aware that you may get the top guns wheeled out for the presentation but more junior practitioners on a day-to-day basis. Be clear as to your expectations and your willingness to pay for them.

SO WHAT NEXT?

Contracts need to be unambiguous and workable for both sides. They should set out timescales, monthly contact meeting arrangements, payment and for what, and approval systems.

Certainly in the early stages of any new relationship as the client you will want to meet relatively frequently with the account handler at the least to ensure everything is kept on track. How often will you meet with the individuals doing the actual work? With whom will they need to be in contact within your organization to ensure they can deliver? The key points to remember are set out in the panel below.

> ### CONTRACTS AND BEYOND
>
> - Who will maintain regular contact?
> - Who approves what?
> - Who will open up the contact networks?
> - When should copy be delivered for consent and returned?
> - When is the finished item to be produced?
> - Who pays for what and when?
> - Duration of contract?
> - Breaking contract?

Consultants need to be kept informed of any changes in personnel on the client side and vice versa. It may be necessary to build in scope for such changes to ensure individuals are brought up to speed.

A contract should be neither too long nor too short in duration. Agreeing to an open-ended period makes imposing checks and balances rather difficult. Anything less than a year will probably not help you deliver consistency – and reviews at the half-yearly stage will enable major problems to be tackled. Quarterly meetings should be used as extended feedback and progress meetings. Clauses should be built in to cope with unexpected circumstances but not misused for trivial issues.

Pay your bills on time and give regular feedback – good as well as not so good. A full bank account is not all that counts.

WORKING WITH SUPPLIERS

The tendering process works particularly well with companies supplying printing and distribution type services too. Be clear in your language and ensure the would-be supplier has actually answered your questions to your satisfaction. Typesetting is often seen as the client's problem, so make sure it is understood this is a required service if necessary.

Photographers, event managers, designers and creatives generally will need to be judged on their previous work. Expect to wade through a lot of portfolios and judge on ability to satisfy similar briefs. With images, remember to secure copyright.

Dot all the i's and cross all the t's in advance so you can concentrate on the more rewarding and interesting aspects of the relationship.

You need to be very clear as to who is picking up the various bills. Allowing a consultancy to buy in specialist services such as print can inflate the bottom line uncomfortably.

A specific time-limited project which is well within the experience and capability of the consultant is relatively easy to cost; less easy can be the ongoing production of a regular publication. Clear guidelines need to be established or costs could escalate out of control with the use of very talented but expensive creative input including photographers.

Here it is worth restating that if you use external photographers it is highly likely they will retain copyright of images produced on your behalf unless you have a contract which states otherwise. Photography can become very expensive if you have to negotiate repeatedly for fresh uses of images and you need to ensure your consultancy appreciates this.

Ideally buy-in should come from as near the top of your organization's management tree as is sensible, depending on the nature of the project. Some chief executives do see it as part of their role to approve all communication; others will want to delegate this.

KEY POINTS TO REMEMBER

- Recognize your actual ability – if you can organize, organize; if you can write, write.
- Check out existing contracts and procedures – change only if you can do or obtain better.
- Talk to other communicators when seeking out contractors.
- Take time in preparing tender documents.
- Give consultancies time to respond to the tender.
- Build in time to give bids proper consideration.
- Aim for a realistically short short-list.
- Make sure there are no distractions on the day the consultancies pitch.
- Contracts need to be practical documents setting out deadlines, meetings, payment, approval system.
- Pay bills on time and give honest feedback.

22

Internal communications – the future

Dear internal communicator – will they need you in 2020 when half the staff are computer-generated images and the other half are robots?

Perhaps you yourself will have half a robot in your arm or a cyber helpmate at your beck and call. It has already been done. Kevin Warwick, Professor of Cybernetics at Reading University, was the first man to have such a computer chip implanted under his skin back in 1999.

Its main use seemed to be opening doors – quite useful when laden down with laptop, papers and the other paraphernalia of modern life, and with your ear glued to your mobile. Perhaps an important advance if the company of 2020 is to avoid lawsuits over repetitive strain injury.

According to Peter Crush writing in *Human Resources* magazine in 2000, the potentially more sinister use of the built-in chip could be a positioning beacon or homing device. You could never get lost but at the same time you could be pinpointed by your boss at all times.

In fact, worryingly, that day may be closer than you think. Mobile phones can already pinpoint you, which might be useful if you are ever accused of a crime you had not committed.

The swipe card that allows you through the barrier to your office could also be used to track your movements. This likely use becomes ever more a probability in these times of heightened security.

And see the Tom Cruise film *Minority Report* as a source for future predictions. Hopefully you will not be arrested in advance of the crime you did not even know you were planning to commit. Just as horrific to some minds would be the opportunity of being hectored by a door frame.

In the film the characters are addressed by name by advertising panels posing as street furniture. The idea of being sold the latest thing in washing powder is bad enough, but being loudly informed of your day's orders smacks rather too much of Big Brother.

In Peter Crush's article, Kevin Warwick has one last distinctly nightmarish vision which should send a collective shiver down the human resources team spine. Will they become redundant? An implant connected to your nervous system could pick up early warning signs of tiredness or pain and measure your stress levels at work. It could then ensure your tailor-made training on how to work more healthily is promptly delivered and your appraisal incorporates its findings.

Enough horror stories for one day. There is sufficient material to be gleaned from current trends to be able to crystal ball gaze without giving everyone nightmares.

But one thing is clear: technology will be a major factor in whatever is to come next in the job, office, media and communications function of the future.

JOB OF THE FUTURE

It takes at least a generation for most predicted change to take place. Back in 1969 management thinker Peter Drucker was predicting that the job for life would be no more. Hardly anyone listened, and just carried on as usual as the ground disappeared from under their feet just as surely as he had predicted.

In The Age of Discontinuity he coined the term 'knowledge worker' to mean a new breed of highly trained, intelligent professional who would feel no obvious loyalty to the organization. Most organizations would now agree that the knowledge worker is the kind of person they want to employ, but that they would like the loyalty added back in.

All sounds positively blissful in the corporate garden apart from the sounds of anguished management trying to hang on to their star players but without the carrot inducements of the past. A role here for the internal communicator?

Ever since the charity Age Concern kicked off what it called the Debate of the Age in the run-up to the millennium, newspapers have been increasingly full of horror stories of pension shortfalls. Some of our silver surfers are apparently going to have to get off the beach and spend longer in the office.

Designing communications programmes to fit the needs of a distant community of not necessarily like-minded individuals including people working from home will pose a challenge for internal communicators.

Large employers are going to continue to contract out their work to other organizations specializing in whatever task it is. Many of those perceived to be working for them will in fact be working for a subcontractor.

Such organizations have to come to terms with an extension of the notion of the internal audience. It can mean their own appointees, former employees of their clients transferred to their workforce, and client-side contacts working for the council itself.

The real difficulty lies in encouraging individuals from very different disciplines, professions, training and education backgrounds to work together as genuine but effectively virtual teams. Internal communication will have to work much more closely with human resources than they may have done in the past.

As internal communication moves further along the communication continuum, away from the distant medium of print towards dialogue, it will have a greater role to play. These largely virtual organizations will have tentacles back into the main employing organizations of the 'team' members. Internal communicators could well find themselves performing an important service to society at large as well as the organization itself by building understanding between disparate practitioners.

More and more industrial sector concerns will be investing in robots and the like to take over the boring, repetitive jobs or even those requiring exceptional precision – neither end of which the human race excels at. This could free existing staff to do more interesting tasks for the same company – or join the dole queue.

Internal communicators will have the task of working with other departments such as human resources to prepare and educate individuals for change in their working lives. The pace of this change is unlikely to slacken as technology provides ever cheaper ways of performing tasks previously carried out by people. Internal communicators may find the content of their work refocused on the human resources or training end of the spectrum.

Information overload is unlikely to lessen. Internal communication professionals will need to develop an understanding of how their people consume and interact with information and so deliver packages to suit.

Technology is often seen as the solution to all problems, but the good times may be some way off and may then only come to the lucky few. Even the unskilled jobs are being farmed out to cheaper places with call centres relocating to other continents where salaries probably would not pay the average British commuter's season ticket. There could be a backlash when consumers find queries mishandled by staff unable to comprehend their concerns. There will be a role here for the internal communicator in helping produce effective training in customer-facing communication skills.

Apparently the experts are unlikely to invent a robot able to prune the roses very effectively, and the cleaning robot requires a house cleared of clutter to start with. So it is likely the demand for these kinds of jobs will continue for a while at least. Perhaps if the domestic cleaning agencies grow large enough they will need internal communicators!

OFFICE OF THE FUTURE

Art and/or artist in the workplace, lawn on the floor instead of carpet, snooker table in the communal area and wine in the fridge. Surely the office of the future is already here.

Apparently service stations are the new meeting areas for many non-deskbound staff, and hotels have wised up to the use to which their reception and bar areas are being put by workers either away from or without an office in the usual sense. These are most likely to provide a setting for informal, cross-organizational grapevines but can also be put to good use by managers overseeing dispersed teams.

Increasing land prices are likely to have more of an impact on where people work in the future. Companies may well downscale their offices and make their staff work from home or in their cars as they move between clients.

In Chapter 11 we looked at communication with such groups as it is conducted now. It would seem they will need more not less support in terms of communication and information. That information will have to be delivered in ways that suits the way they work. So it is likely that communication programmes may be designed to meet the needs of different staff groups rather than the old one size fits all solutions of yesteryear.

Implications for the internal communication function itself include scope for larger teams of specialists tackling very specific duties – change management, website and publication production, communications skills training. The last item would be particularly important where managers overseeing front-line and other staff require better training and improved support materials in order to deliver communication programmes themselves. The internal communicator of the future is likely to take on even more the guise of the facilitator rather than the producer.

NEW MEDIA OF THE FUTURE

If history is any kind of guide whatever, it is more than likely that the older communications vehicles we have today will still be with us in some guise for some time to come. Radio did not sound the death-knell of newspapers and television did not kill off either. Theatre was widely touted as on its last legs when cinema hoved into view 100 years ago, and that in its turn has not withered with the arrival of video and now DVD. Most seem to thrive, but often as hybrids.

What is likely is a greater convergence of technologies. Third generation mobile phones (or 3G as they are more popularly known), provide better-quality images and speed of delivery. The addition of larger keypads and even quicker connections could result in mini video conferences coming back on the menu. Staff needing to access information or transmit it should be able to do this more quickly than previously. All this will boost communication with the dispersed workforce.

Print publications now rarely accept hard-copy prints of photographs except for obituary columns. Digital technology has certainly revolutionized the way images can be transmitted. A major manufacturer in the camera and film sector has announced that it will concentrate its efforts on digital devices from now on.

Ambient media – the talking doorway referred to earlier – could be another way forward. It may seem less visually intrusive in some ways than posters plastered on every mat, step and wall and every other available space. However, managing competing noises in the workplace will become an increasing issue and you may see a greater use of ear pieces.

Information overload or communication overload is unlikely to become less of a problem in spite of new ways to manage information. The only way to tackle this is to ensure staff know how to use their time and technology properly to keep the mass of data under control. Some companies, often the technology ones themselves, have limited the use of mobile phones to office hours only and banned texting on particular days. This is not necessarily all that altruistic, as they feel staff are missing out on face-to-face interaction and there is a cost involved in the time spent tackling e-mails.

Businesses will continue to try to persuade their expensive assets (the workforce) to share their knowledge with their colleagues through knowledge management schemes. But until staff can see a benefit to themselves rather than the management, information hoarding is likely to continue to be the tendency. Many fear handing over a lifetime's experience will have one result – a pointer in the direction of the door marked 'exit'. Overcoming that lack of trust will be a major task for the internal communicator of the near future.

FUNCTION OF THE FUTURE

So robots aside, where does that leave the internal communications function over the next few years? Well, you too could be replaced by a machine. There are already computer programs that can generate a media release and there will apparently be software capable of the journalist's job by 2020. So that is the writing out of the way.

Systems also exist which can provide the framework for putting together a communication strategy. There are communications planning tools which can be used to train middle managers and non-specialists in the various stages of a communications plan so that they can deliver these much more effectively.

These tools take them through the process of identifying the audiences, establishing what they are trying to communicate and the key messages. A touch of the button then provides the recommended course of action including the communications channels to be used. Hopefully this would be done in conjunction with the communication adviser that you will have become.

Nick Helsby (2002) in his report on the future of the internal communication function suggests that there is a need to escape the implementation trap and to move to the advisory role in order to advance the cause higher up the organization. However, managers still seem to prize doers rather than thinkers in this area.

Teams are certainly likely to continue to shrink and the only way a global telecommunications organization like NTL could have reduced its internal communication headcount from 40 to 6 was by pushing tasks closer to where the intended audience is sited. But there is still a need for a central function to produce a print publication three times a year to provide a context for the information that goes out constantly online. Face-to-face communication is unlikely to go away – in fact its popularity seems to grow year on year – but it is likely the supporting technology will carry on evolving to provide more dramatic and useful props.

Legislation could well increase the influence of the internal communicator, particularly that emanating from Europe and requiring true involvement of the workforce. Other examples include the Working Time Directive which sought to limit the working week. This piece of legislation has been largely ignored in the UK but a possible tightening up from the European centre may change that.

Discrimination legislation will also herald further changes to content and approach as a more diverse workforce begins to take shape. Some human resources practitioners fear they may well end up simply ticking the appropriate boxes and becoming paper-pushers.

There is no reason for the internal communicator to suffer that fate. In fact the changes already coming provide a welcome opportunity to demonstrate the practitioner's finely tuned skills in audience and message segmentation.

Helsby's view of the future is that some things will stay the same – there will always be a need for someone to manage the communications channels such as the intranet, newsletter, videos and publications.

Certain industrial sectors, particularly retail and services, will continue to prize the more highly skilled practitioners and these will become more valued translating to fatter pay cheques.

It is not especially clear where internal communication might end up. At present, as the Helsby report demonstrates, many practitioners are situated in the corporate communication department but there are pockets in human resources, marketing and elsewhere. A more holistic approach involving the various departments in a more seamless manner may be the best way forward but may prove too radical for most.

A new style of leadership as demonstrated by reports produced by the Council for Excellence in Management and Leadership (Fox *et al*, 2001; Perren and Grant, 2001) may create a demand for a new style of communicator with more of an advisory role with a reporting line to the CEO.

So where does technology fit into all this?

TECHNOLOGY – PLATFORM OR DRIVER?

Probably it will be a bit of both in the internal communication world of the near future. It is definitely up to the practitioners themselves to seize the opportunities as they come up so that they are in charge of the technology rather than the technology being in charge of them, as has so often appeared to be the case in recent years.

MEDIAMaker's Operations Director, David Coe, believes empowerment will become a real force to be reckoned with. 'You have heard of customer relational management, the one-to-one relationship with the customer, well how about erm – employee relational management.'

He believes that in order to empower the employee they need 'to feel part of a growing organization that is communicating. Personalise everything so when they log on it is filtered. That takes something from external marketing – viral marketing techniques.' Perhaps viral communications could become the electronic version of the grapevine which the internal communications team could tap into, participate in or use. Ignoring the grapevine will not be an option as the wrong sort of information could be spread far faster than ever before.

Although David Coe concedes there is a possibility of Big Brother elements creeping in, used in the right way computer-mediated communication is a very powerful tool. Intranets allow anyone to put a question to the top and theoretically get an answer.

He sees video being used in different ways, courtesy of webstreaming. Although video could go straight to the individual's desktop, motivational material might be better presented to groups. Technology will assist the communicator in making the choice of delivery.

Technology will also bring a new lease of life to some tired old media. It is possible to mimic the best of external media with the aid of print technology. Publications have been given a new lease of life and new relevance by taking a leaf out of the regionalization or editionalization that is common to both national and local print media in Britain. They have also been able to run the copy in different languages too.

3G technology will also allow individuals to access much more information more quickly while on the move. This is likely to be facilitated rather more smoothly by the fourth generation of phones currently under development, according to Bob Schukai of Motorola. Mobile technology can also be used to pinpoint staff so the control elements can be extended to staff outside the physical boundaries of the central office.

Some companies are already putting text messaging to good use to alert their mobile workforces to important news. It has also been useful in triggering urgent cascade briefings particularly about price sensitive information.

MEDIAMaker believes texting is still in its infancy and has some way to go. David Coe sees largely untapped potential in the field of measurement surveys. It is possible to use texting as a polling mechanism, a sort of mechanized tick box – one click, one vote!

But do not wait for someone else to take the lead in engaging the workforce, otherwise the time that the internal communication function could really make its mark might have come and gone unnoticed. Every threat is after all a challenge in disguise, and technology is but a tool to be put to good use for a better future.

The final word also goes to David Coe who urges everyone to 'look to what is happening externally for what will be done internally in terms of communication in the future'.

Appendix 1

Internal communications knowledge and skills

A joint working party made up of the Chartered Institute of Public Relations' Internal Communication Alliance, Communicators in Business, the International Association of Business Communicators and the Internal Communication Association has been looking at a range of issues.

One of the most important of these is establishing the levels of skills, knowledge and training internal communicators need at various stages of their professional life. A skills matrix has been produced which covers both generic business and management as well as the more specific internal communication competencies. Courses are not included as there is a plethora of providers out there.

BAND 1 (ENTRY LEVEL 6–12 MONTHS)

Graduate in the process of learning core skills and gaining basic knowledge in the wider context of communications and management.

Generic business and management

Knowledge

- basics of management theory and practice relevant to sector of operation;
- legal issues – health and safety legislation, etc.

Skills

- time management;
- meeting practices;
- team working;
- networking;
- desk research;
- interpersonal communication;
- specialist – corporate and internal communication.

Knowledge

- what internal communication is;
- the politics of communication;
- planning basics – audiences, messages, media, etc.

Skills

- the basics of writing and editing (proofreading, grammar, style, plain English);
- working with clients (internal/external) and suppliers;
- photography and design basics.

Direct experience

- working as an assistant or junior team member;
- supporting colleagues in the delivery of communication campaigns;
- exposure to a variety of channels and techniques;
- basic news and feature writing for a variety of channels.

BAND 2 (12 MONTHS–2/3 YEARS)

Becoming an effective practitioner, growing skills set, deepening understanding of business/management and internal communications.

Generic business and management

Knowledge

- finance for non-financial managers;
- management agenda (quality, Investors in People, etc);
- communication and leadership – communication competencies, role of leaders, etc.

Skills

- negotiation skills;
- assertiveness;
- interpersonal skills (consulting techniques);
- presentation techniques;
- basic project management;
- budget setting and control.

Specialist – corporate and internal communication

Knowledge

- planning simple internal communications programmes;
- role and benefits of face-to-face communications;
- awareness of wider communications disciplines (PR, marketing communications, etc);
- knowledge and understanding of professional codes of practice;
- relationship between human resources, internal communication and marketing;
- role of research and measurement in internal communication practice;
- law;
- psychology in the workplace;
- selection and evaluation of different internal communication media;
- how internal communications links to business strategy.

Skills

- writing and sub-editing newsletters, intranet (including news and features);
- interviewing for publication and research;
- sub-editing colleagues' work;

- planning simple programmes/campaigns (including audience segmentation);
- providing tactical advice to managers on communications practice;
- conducting limited scope research projects;
- simple facilitation skills for research and planning meetings;
- developing personal networks;
- organizing and running events and conferences;
- visual identity and brand management.

Direct experience

- regular writing and sub-editing for variety of formats/media;
- managing range of internal communication channels (projects and continuous);
- conducting small-scale qualitative and quantitative research projects;
- developing simple campaigns to defined objectives;
- working with colleagues on human resources issues;
- working with colleagues from corporate communications and marketing backgrounds;
- organizing and running a range of events (conferences, roadshows, workshops).

BAND 3 (MANAGER/SUPERVISOR 2–3 YEARS POSTGRADUATE EXPERIENCE)

Generic business and management

Knowledge

- financial and strategic planning;
- branding;
- human resource management.

Skills

- delegation and supervision;
- managing conflict;
- influencing skills;
- managing a budget;
- facilitation skills.

Specialist – corporate and internal communication

Knowledge

- mastery of management theory and practice relevant to sector;
- planning complex internal communications programmes;
- good practice in people management and budgeting;
- knowledge and understanding of codes of practice;
- law and how it relates to people management and communications;
- evaluation of internal communications good practice;
- organization culture and change management;
- risk and incident management – the role of internal communications.

Skills

- specifying and managing suppliers including negotiations and account management;
- maintaining internal networks;
- coaching and leading small teams;
- coaching managers on communications programmes;
- speech writing;
- improving organizational communication flow – development of e-mail guidelines, policies, etc;
- developing and delivering complex projects;
- planning and managing detailed research projects;
- facilitation skills for research and planning meetings;
- supporting change projects;
- alignment of internal and external communication programmes.

Direct experience

- developing new or existing communication channels;
- delivering complex projects;
- managing external suppliers (designers, AV, consultants);
- commissioning and reviewing qualitative and quantitative research projects;
- developing communication campaigns to meet defined objectives;
- involvement in multidisciplinary project teams;
- working in environments where a number of cultures need to be managed;
- working with colleagues from corporate communications or marketing backgrounds;
- working on projects at time of crisis or rapid change;

- planning long-term communications programme for large organization;
- experience delivering programmes concerning brands, values and behaviours, restructuring, cultural change.

BAND 4 (SENIOR PRACTITIONER)

Leading department or consulting practice providing support to senior managers.

Generic business and management

Knowledge

- understanding key functions and issues faced (marketing, finance, human resources);
- deep sector expertise and knowledge;
- keeping abreast of current thinking and good practice in management in and out of the sector;
- business ethics;
- motivation and leadership.

Skills

- leading and inspiring a team;
- coaching individuals;
- human resource planning and management;
- advanced negotiation skills;
- advanced facilitation skills.

Specialist – corporate and internal communication

Knowledge

- knowledge and understanding of codes of practice;
- translating complex business requirements into internal communications programmes;
- good practice in people management and budgeting.

Skills

- leading department or consulting team including providing development and coaching for junior team members;
- managing complex relationships with suppliers;
- working with and counselling very senior leaders;
- managing in multiple cultures;
- use of advanced tools and techniques – appreciative inquiry, storytelling etc;
- internal branding – making the links between internal and external communication;
- conducting internal communication audits.

Direct experience

- leader of organizational change programmes;
- development of internal communication strategy;
- regular exposure to senior leadership team/board;
- developing strong coalitions with other functions (marketing, human resources, finance).

Appendix 2

Communications in the public sector – a snapshot

The public sector is often seen as one amorphous mass, but it is a much more complex environment affected by its reporting lines to politicians, be they in local or central government. Many of the activities previously deemed to be the role of the local monolith are just as likely to have been outsourced, and local authorities have correspondingly shrivelled in size, at least in terms of front-line staff. This appendix will look at local government in particular.

Local councils have to balance the demands of locally elected councillors who may or may not be in the ruling coalition. Policy can shift radically on the sudden vacation of a seat. This has certainly happened in councils where there has been no substantial majority. Gaining consensus on the management view on service and policy issues which may hit staffing levels can be just as tortuous as launching any announcement to the Stock Exchange.

The sector has been taking an increasing interest in internal communication as pressure is brought to bear by central government wishing to deliver on election promises. With that interest has come the appearance of consultancies that specialize in the field, and one such adviser said there had been an increased investment in internal communications on behalf of local authorities. Councils are often employers of literally thousands of people, many of whom live locally and so are truly ambassadors. Techniques from the commercial sector such as staff roadshows are becoming more prevalent and there is a growing emphasis on measurement of results over time.

More than 2 million people work in local government. In his study of local government internal communications (2002) Paul Inglefield, Head of Performance and Organization Development at Adur District Council, received a creditable near 50 per cent response to his survey of all authorities.

More than half the respondents said that internal communications is managed by corporate communications while 14 per cent said it was not managed at all!

Some 91 per cent use team briefings and 85 per cent use conferences or briefings. A staff newsletter is produced by 89 per cent, mostly at least quarterly in frequency.

Local authorities are not so good on the research and evaluation of programmes but that may be indicative of the fairly recent arrival of internal communication in the sector.

At the time of the survey 12 per cent of respondents did not have an intranet. Corporate communications functions in 12 per cent of cases have responsibility for the intranet, but 40 per cent share the task with IT and 32 per cent have no input at all.

Communications departments vary enormously in size. Just under a fifth have more than nine full-time staff with communications as the main focus of work, with the bulk (32 per cent) having just one or two full-timers. But 10 per cent of all authorities reported they had no member of staff with responsibility for communications either internal or external.

Just 12 per cent spend more than 30 per cent of their time on internal communications while the bulk (40 per cent) earmarked no more than 10 per cent. A worrying 16 per cent spent none of their communications budget on internal communications, 58 per cent spent less than 10 per cent, while only 7 per cent devoted just under a third.

Nearly a quarter of all authorities carry out a full staff survey every year but 16 per cent had never surveyed their staff at all. However, it could be they are assessing views in other ways, as 47 per cent said they use focus groups and 70 per cent workshops or seminars to establish staff views.

There is no need to get complacent, as nearly half those asked said that less than 50 per cent of their staff felt that the council communicated well with them. A slightly lower percentage felt that less than half their staff understood the organization's aims and objectives.

Top management seemed to be equally divided as to the importance of internal communications. However, senior echelons of the authority seemed largely invisible with respondents reporting that nearly 70 per cent of top managers do not or rarely 'walk the job'.

There were country differences in responsibility for internal communications. Scottish unitary authorities reported that internal communications is managed by corporate communications in 71 per cent of cases. The figure overall was 56 per cent but only 33 per cent for Northern Ireland. In the London boroughs a quarter report that human resources manages internal communications.

Just a third of councils have a strategy for internal communication and a similar percentage says it is updated every year. Some 42 per cent of heads of communications describe their role as that of senior adviser to the decision makers. Approximately 27 per cent said they had full responsibility for internal communications programmes and made policy decisions. Just under a third described themselves in terms of products (newsletters). However, 16 per cent of heads of communication are at board or corporate management team level.

Communications training is seen as important not just for managers but also for staff. It is not clear whether this kind of activity enables practitioners to take on a more advisory role or in fact be replaced at the front line. Broader findings suggest councils that practise two-way communications are more likely to have more contented staff and in turn more satisfied residents.

Appendix 3

Setting up an internal communications function – things to consider

Perhaps surprisingly there are still large organizations which have as yet to formalize their systems for internal communications.

The following is intended as a checklist for practitioners setting up an internal communication function from scratch. It takes the form of a series of questions to be considered.

Who will be your top-level sponsor?

Even if you do not have a seat on the board or a direct line to the CEO you need a senior director to take on the responsibility for internal communication. It shows the organization they understand the importance of the function to the organization.

How will you get the backing of the next level down?

You need to build relationships with directors/heads of functions key to the internal communication function – these include planning, corporate communication, human resources and marketing as the minimum.

Do you know how well the organization is actually performing?

Build a good understanding of the company's financial position and develop arguments to show how the internal communication function will help the bottom line.

What tools are already being used?

Look at what is already in place in terms of meetings, publications, websites, etc. Establish how often they take place/are published/updated/refreshed. Look at the state of the content – just how interesting and relevant is it?

What is missing?

Find out if employees are getting the information tripod they need to do their jobs, ie information top down (from the board and senior management for the big picture), bottom up (feedback: how are their views captured and given to the board?) and sideways (across functions and, dare we say it, silos).

Do employees actually attend, read, watch, interact with the media offered?

Elicit employee views on existing communication channels and vehicles. What would they really like in order to perform their duties to the optimum? Set up a regular means of auditing both the individual aspects of your communication strategy and the totality.

What do your competitors do?

Compare what is already offered by your organization with similar bodies against which you would normally be benchmarked. Do they do it better, or is their approach different for a reason?

What issues bug management and employees?

Ask directors, senior managers and employees what really irritates them about the way the organization currently works and how this might be corrected through communication.

Can the organization afford what you have in mind?

Prepare a budget that meets the communication needs of both management and employees. Build up your argument for winning the funds by demonstrating how your plans will add to the bottom line.

Is there anyone currently fulfilling some internal communication duties?

Even if there has been no clearly established function it is more than likely that an intranet is being run out of IT or a newsletter thrown together by the CEO's PA. You need to get these people on board when you are either putting some process into what they do so it fits into the big picture, relieving them of their duties or otherwise obtaining their support.

If you work for a decentralized organization, how will you keep internal communication consistent and coherent across the different parts?

Set up a network of people with responsibility for internal communication. They do not need to be professional communicators; they do need the support of their management (See Chapter 18).

Do you really want to provide the function single-handed?

Establish your expertise deficit, your personal one and that of any existing practitioners in the organization. Decide what is best done in-house, and what best outsourced. Ensure you have your financial arguments lined up to show you can bridge the gaps you have identified.

Are existing suppliers any good?

Review all supplier relationships and only keep the ones that work and are cost effective within your new budget, not the old one. Make sure your tendering programme for any replacements is realistic.

When will it all happen?

Establish a timescale you can work to that is realistic. Do not over-promise but do not keep everyone waiting too long for results.

How will you establish the elements of the strategy and their specific contents?

Consult the front-line staff as well as their managers and directors to formulate a relevant communication programme.

How will you demonstrate that added value you keep going on about?

Build in effective evaluation mechanisms and make sure they are costed in the budget.

Appendix 4

Useful addresses

The following are organizations supporting individuals working in internal communication. Where available, websites have been given or e-mail contacts.

Internal Communication Alliance
Sectoral group of the Chartered Institute of Public Relations
website: www.cipr.co.uk then go to sectoral group and select Internal Communication Alliance

International Association of Business Communicators
website: www.iabc.com

Communicators in Business (British Association of Communicators in Business)
website: www.cib.uk.com

Internal Communication Association
A special interest group of the Work Foundation (previously Industrial Society)
www.theworkfoundation.com

The Work Foundation (formerly Industrial Society) www.thework foundation.com

International Visual Communication Association (IVCA) www.ivca.org

Institute of Sales Promotion www.isp.org.uk

References

Alexander III, E, Penley, L and Jernigan, I (1991) The effect of individual difference on managerial media choice, *Management Communication Quarterly*, **5**, (2) pp 155–73

Ali, M (1999) *The DIY Guide to Public Relations* (2nd edn), Directory of Social Change, London

Arnott, M (1986) Effective employee communication, Unpublished paper

Ashford, D (2001) Public relations or human resource management? An investigation into the responsibility for employee communication with UK organisations, MA in Public Relations

Boyle, D (2001) *The Tyranny of Numbers: Why counting can't make us happy*, HarperCollins

Brandon, M (1997) From the three Bs to the high Cs, *Communication World*, April/May, US

Brosius, H and Wermann, G (1996) Who sets the agenda: agenda setting as two step-flow, *Communication Research*, **23**, (5)

Center, A and Jackson, P (1995) *Public Relations Practices: Managerial case studies and problems*, Prentice-Hall, Englewood Cliffs, NJ

Clampitt, P (1991) *Communicating for Managerial Effectiveness*, Sage, London

Clutterbuck, D (1997) Why measure? and What to measure, *Handbook of Internal Communication*, ed E Scholes, Gower, Aldershot, pp 271–82

Crush, P (2000) From e-hr to eternity, *Human Resources*, August

Cutlip, S Center, A and Broom, G (1985) *Effective Public Relations*, 7th edn, Prentice-Hall, Englefield Cliffs, NJ

Drucker, P (1969) *The Age of Discontinuity*, Heinemann, London

Fiske, J (1992)*Introduction to Communication Studies*, 2nd edn, Routledge, London

Foster, J (2001) *Effective Writing Skills for Public Relations*, 2nd edn, Kogan Page, London

Fox, S *et al* (2001) *The Nature and Quality of Management and Leadership in the Professions: A Qualitative Study*, Council for Excellence in Management and Leadership, London

Gaymer, J (2003) Whistleblowing law widens its protective net, *Human Resources*, February

Gorman, B (2003) Employee engagement after two decades of change, *Strategic Communication Management*, 7 (1)

Gregory, A (2004) *Public Relations in Practice*, 2nd edn, Kogan Page, London

Hacker, K (1996) Missing links in the evolution of electronic democratization, *Media, Culture and Society*, 18, pp 213–32

Hacker, K *et al* (1998) Employee attitudes regarding electronic mail policies, a case study, *Management Communication Quarterly*, 11 (3), pp 422–52

Handy, C (1985) *Understanding Organizations*, Penguin, London

Helsby, N (2002) *The Rise of the Internal Communicator: A research report on the role of senior internal communication practitioners conducted in 37 major UK and US businesses*, Watson Helsby, London

Howard, W (1988) *The Practice of Public Relations*, Heinemann, London

Hutton, P (2004) Survey reveals the power of internal communication, *Profile*, 46 (Nov/Dec), Chartered Institute of Public Relations, London, p 15

Inglefield, P (2002) A comparative study into internal communications in local government, MA in Public Communication

McQuail, D (1992) *Mass Communication Theory*, Sage, London

Nathan, M with Doyle, J (2002) *Workspace: The final frontier*, Industrial Society, London

O'Sullivan, T *et al* (1992) *Key Concepts in Communication*, Routledge, London

Perren, L and Grant, P (2001) *Management and Leadership in UK SMEs Witness testimonies from the world of entrepreneurs and SME managers*, Council for Excellence in Management and Leadership, London

Phillips, D (2001) *Online Public Relations*, Kogan Page, London

Quirke, B (2002) Managers must convey the big picture, *Professional Manager*, May

Reed, M (1997) Audits, *Handbook of Internal Communication*, ed E Scholes, Gower, Aldershot

Smythe, J (1995) Organisational communication – the disciple emerges, *Smythe Dorward Lambert Review* (London), Aug, pp 1–2

Smythe, J (May 2002) The rise and fall of the internal communicator, *Profile*, Chartered Institute of Public Relations, London

Varey, R (1997) Understanding how communication works, *Handbook of Internal Communications*, ed E Scholes, Gower, Aldershot, pp 219–34

Welsh, T and Greenwood, W (2003) *Essential Law for Journalists*, 17th edn, Oxford University Press

Williams, K (1989) *Behavioural Aspects of Marketing*, Heinemann, Oxford

Wilson, R Thomas-Derrick, A and Wright, P (2001) What globalization means for communication, *Strategic Communication Management*, October/November

Windahl, S, Signitzer, B and Olson, J (1993) *Using Communication Theory*, Sage, London

Winter, M (2002) Maintaining stability through corporate change at Prudential UK, *Strategic Communication Management*, **6** (4)

Work Foundation (2002) Internal communications, *Managing Best Practice No 100*, Working paper

Yates, J and Orlikowski, W (1992) Genres of organizational communication: a structurational approach to studying communication and media, *Academy of Management Review*, **17** (2), pp 299–326

Further reading

BOOKS

Argenti, P (2003) *Corporate Communication*, 3rd edn, McGraw Hill, London

Arnold, J, Cooper, L and Robertson, I (1995) *Work Psychology: Understanding human behaviour in the workplace*, Pitman, London

Baker, S and K (1998) *The Complete Idiot's Guide to Project Management*, Alpha Books, New York

Belbin, R (1996) *Management Teams, Why Do They Succeed or Fail?*, Heinemann, London

Buchanan, D and Boddy, D (1992) *The Expertise of the Change Agent*, Prentice Hall, London

Burke, W (1994) *Organization Development: A process of learning and change*, Addison Wesley

Collins, J and C J (2002) *From Good to Great*, Robson, London

Collins, J and Porras, T (2000) *Built to Last*, Random House Business, London

Covey, S (1994) *First Things First: To live, to love, to learn , to leave a legacy*, Simon & Shuster, London

Deetz, S, Tracy, S and Simpson, J (2000) *Leading Organizations through Transition*, Sage, London

Eden, C and Ackermann, F (1998) *Making Strategy*, Sage, London

Evans, H (2000) *Essential English for Journalists, Editors and Writers*, Crawford Gillam, London

Frank, A and Brownell, J (1989) *Organizational Communication and Behaviour,* Holt, Rinehard & Winston, New York

Freeman, R (1984) *Strategic Management: A stakeholder approach,* Pitman, London

Goyder, M (1998) *Living Tomorrow's Company,* Gower, Aldershot

Gratton, L (2000) *Living Strategy: Putting people at the heart of corporate purpose,* Prentice Hall, London

Handy, C (1994) *The Empty Raincoat,* Hutchinson, London

Ind, N (2001) *Living the Brand: How to transform every member of your organisation into a brand champion,* Kogan Page, London

Isaacs, W (1999) *The Art of Dialogue,* Bantam Books

Jensen, B (2000) *Simplicity: The new competitive advantage in a world of more, better, faster,* HarperCollins Business, London

Johnson (1999) *Who Moved my Cheese? An amazing way to deal with change in your work,* Vermilion, London

Knight, S (2002) *NLP at Work,* Nicholas Brealey, London

Kotter, J (1996) *Leading Change,* Harvard Business Press

Larkin, T and Larkin, S (1994) *Communicating Change,* McGraw-Hill, New York

Lewis, R (2000) *When Cultures Collide,* Nicholas Brealey, London

McQuail, D and Windahl, S (1981) *Communications Models,* Longman, London

Mintzberg, H (1979) *The Structuring of Organizations,* Prentice Hall, London

Murray, D (1995) *Knowledge Machines,* Longman, London

Peters, T and Waterman, R (1982) *In Search of Excellence,* Harper & Row, London

Pringle, H and Gordon, W (2001) *Brand Manners: How to create the self confident organization to live the brand,* Wiley, Chichester

Quirke, B (1996) *Communicating Corporate Change,* McGraw-Hill, London

Quirke, B (2002) *Making the Connections: Using internal communication to turn strategy into action,* Gower, Aldershot

Rees, W (2001) *The Skills of Management,* 5th edn, Thomson Learning

Robbins, H and Finley, M (1997) *Why Change Doesn't Work: Why initiatives go wrong and how to try again and succeed,* Orion Business, London

Rousseau, D (1995) *Psychological Contracts in Organisations,* Sage, London

Schein, E (1999) *Corporate Culture Survival Guide,* Prentice Hall, Hemel Hempstead

Schultz, M, Hatch, M and Larsen, M (2000) *The Expressive Organization,* Oxford University Press

Sellers, L (1968) *Doing it in Style,* Pergamon, Oxford

Stone, D, Patton, B and Heen, S (1999) *Difficult Conversations: How to discuss what matters most,* Michael Joseph, London

Tuck, M (1976) *How do we choose? A study in behaviour,* Methuen, London

Weick, K (1995) *Sensemaking in organizations,* Sage, London

Woodward, H and Buchholz, S (1987) *Aftershock: Helping people through corporate change*, Wiley

JOURNALS/PERIODICALS

Business Communicator
Communication Research
European Journal of Communication
Harvard Business Review
Human Communication Research
Human Resources
Journal of Business and Technical Communication
Journal of Communication Management
Management Communication Quarterly
Management Today
PR Week
Profile (CIPR)
Strategic Communication Management

Index